How to be the best
at your favorite games

BEAT
THE
GAME!

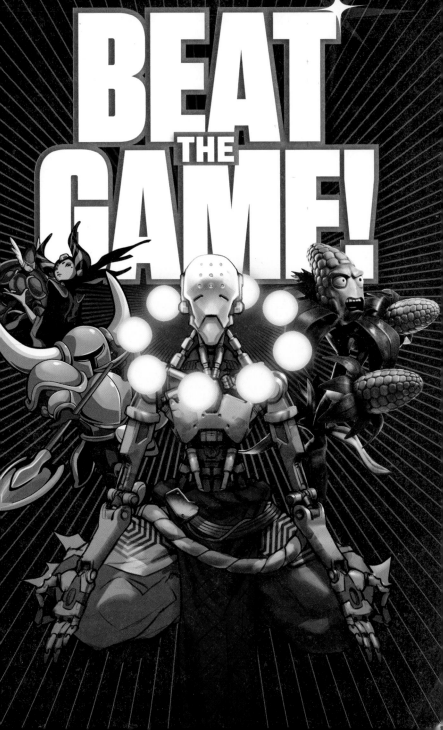

EDITOR IN CHIEF
Jon White

EDITOR
Stephen Ashby

WRITERS
Luke Albigés, Wesley Copeland, Jonathan Gordon, Ross Hamilton, Oliver Hill, Ryan King, Simon Miller, Dominic Peppiatt, Dominic Reseigh-Lincoln, Edward Smith, Paul Walker-Emig, Josh West

LEAD DESIGNER
Adam Markiewicz

DESIGNERS
Andy Downes, Andy Salter, Liam Warr, Jonathan Wells

PRODUCTION
Sarah Bankes, Sanne de Boer, Steve Holmes, Fiona Hudson, Jen Neal

NO MAN'S SKY

WHY NOT TAKE A TRIP ACROSS A GALAXY OF OVER 18 QUINTILLION PLANETS? GET THE BEST TIPS AND TRICKS ON PAGE 36 ...

STAYING SAFE AND HAVING FUN

As with any gaming, check out a game's rating before you play it, and if you're playing online with others, remember that they're not real-life friends. Here are some top tips:

1. Talk to your parents about what the rules are in your family, such as how long you can play games for, or what websites you can visit.

2. Don't download or install games or apps to any device, or fill out any forms on the Internet, without first checking with the person that the device belongs to.

3. Take regular breaks— putting your mobile device down every now and then is not only good for your eyes, it will also allow you to refresh and improve your play.

4. If you're playing games when you're on the move, be aware of other people, and look where you're going.

5. Don't forget—games are meant to be fun! If things aren't going well in the game, just take a timeout and come back to it later.

6. Don't respond to any online conversations that are mean or make you feel bad. Let your parents know right away.

7. Never agree to meet someone you met online in person, and never send photographs of yourself.

8. Don't feel pressured to spend money on games or apps. If a game tells you to spend money, speak to your parents.

9. When you're online, be nice to other people. Don't say or do anything that could hurt someone else's feelings or make them feel unhappy.

10. Never give out personal information such as your real name, phone number, password, or anything about your parents.

CONTENTS

FEATURES

GAME SERIES

42

38

QUICK TIPS & TRICKS

114

WELCOME TO BEAT THE GAME!

MASTER YOUR FAVORITE GAMES

Video games are all about having fun, whether you're playing alone or with friends. But the more you play them, the more you can't help wanting to be really awesome at them! Unfortunately, there always seems to be a tricky level, tough boss, or epic challenge standing in your way.

So, we've put together this book, packed full of hints, tips, and cheats to help you improve your all-around gaming skills and be the best at even the most challenging games. Find out how to get past the hardest levels, take down the biggest bosses, and unlock every Trophy and Achievement.

We've also spoken to some of the best gamers in the world to get their pro tips and tricks. Their advice will improve your strategy, and help you learn when to be patient, when to go all-out, and when you might need a little help from your friends.

Most importantly, they will show you that even the very best players have to work hard and practice to reach the top of their game.

We've covered all the coolest, toughest, craziest, and most popular games. So whether you're still in the hunt for your first Trophy, or you've already got a huge Gamerscore, we can help. Don't let your favorite games beat you—read on and learn how to beat them . . .

82

HOW TO BECOME A BETTER GAMER

GETTING THE MOST OUT OF YOUR HARDWARE

XBOX ONE

If you have one of the latest Xbox One S models, you can enjoy 4K video and HDR gaming on compatible TVs, to give you the ultimate gaming experience. Xbox gamers can also power up their consoles with a Kinect sensor, and use voice commands to take control.

TABLET

If you're an Achievement or Trophy hunter, a tablet can be really helpful. Use it to gain quick access to video walkthroughs, and websites like XboxAchievements.com. You might also find that some of your favorite games have mobile versions available to download on tablet, too.

CONTROLLERS

You can customize controllers with special grips and casings, which can give you the edge when playing against friends. Keep your controllers in good condition, and make sure they're always fully charged.

They says that practice makes perfect, but to be the very best gamer you can be, it take a bit more. It takes determination, as you plug away at the toughest games. It takes skill, as you perfect moves and combos that only the nimblest fingers can perform. It takes guts, as you take risks to gain an advantage. It takes a cool head, as you stay calm, while others might panic. It takes not being afraid to ask for help when you need it. And that's what this book is for . . .

KINECT

Xbox One gamers can use this as a microphone during games, and it allows you to record the moment you unlock an Achievement by shouting "Xbox, record that!" Some games can also only be played through Kinect, such as *Kinect Sports Rivals*. It's not essential, but Kinect makes a great addition to your setup.

TV

Any TV will play your favorite games. However, larger screens will allow you to pick out more details. You may have heard about 4K or HDR TV. You really don't need these features to enjoy your gaming, but if you have a TV with these features, you can connect an Xbox One S or PS4 Pro to make the most of them.

LAPTOP

When Achievement or Trophy hunting, you might want to consider having a guide open as you play. Video walkthroughs or detailed guides on XboxAchievements.com make for excellent companions, and a laptop is a great way to keep lots of guides open at once.

PS4

Sony's console has cross-play with the PS Vita, so if you own both consoles you can play PS4 games on the small screen when you're at home. The latest console in the family, the PS4 Pro, gives players the chance to play 4K games thanks to more powerful internal hardware. However, even the standard PS4 will pump out HD games and play Blu-rays.

BE THE ULTIMATE GAMER

WHAT ARE ACHIEVEMENTS AND TROPHIES?

So, you've completed *Mighty No. 9.* You've gained a 20-player killstreak in *Overwatch*. You've shut the opposition out on *Rocket League*. Good job! But how will everyone else know how awesome you are? You need proof of your incredible gaming exploits, and that's where Achievements and Trophies come in.

Every Xbox game offers Achievements on completion of certain challenges, while every PlayStation game offers Trophies. These completed challenges are indicators of your gaming feats, displayed alongside your Gamertag (on Xbox) or PSN name (on PlayStation). They are an instant way of telling the world how good you are at gaming.

Each Achievement is worth a certain Gamerscore value. The higher your overall Gamerscore, the better your reputation. The same goes for PlayStation, which awards a Platinum Trophy to anyone who completes every challenge in a game. The more Platinums a gamer has, the better at gaming they are. Obviously.

So, how can *you* earn these Achievements or Trophies? When you load a game for the first time, all you have to do is check the Achievements or Trophies tab to see them all. As you complete the challenges, you will get notifications on-screen showing that you have unlocked one! There may even be some secret Trophies and Achievements to find—but don't worry, we've got these covered.

Did you know?

The first Xbox games with Achievements included *FIFA 06*, *Amped 3*, and *Kameo: Elements of Power*.

WHAT'S THE REAL DIFFERENCE BETWEEN COMPLETING A GAME AND 100% COMPLETING A GAME?

Completing a game means getting to the end credits. The final boss has fallen, the world has been saved, and the hero is being carried off to glory by a cheering crowd. But just completing a game isn't enough any more. To really show off, you have to 100% complete a game: This means gaining every Achievement or Trophy the game has to offer. In doing so, you have more than reached the end credits. You've also beaten the game on the hardest difficulty level, or with one life, or without saving, or whatever you've been asked to do. And that means you're definitely among the best.

WHO ARE THE BEST?
▶ Stallion83   Hakoom

The best gamers have long been established on Xbox and PlayStation. Stallion83 is the king of Xbox, having been the first gamer to hit 1 million Gamerscore and received personal congratulations from Microsoft. And he hasn't slowed down since then. The American gamer is rocketing towards an impressive 1.5 million Gamerscore. On the PlayStation side it's Hakoom who dominates, with over 1,000 Platinums to his name. That means he's fully completed over 1,000 games. So, now you know what you're up against . . .

HOW GOOD ARE YOU?

You can see how you compare against your friends on either console by looking at their profile. This will list all the Achievements and Trophies they have unlocked, so you know how you match up

against them, and can try to beat their high scores. However, you won't see the secret challenges unless you have also unlocked them. You can also compare your success with other players through Xbox.com and PlayStation.com.

TOP GAMING TECHNIQUES

DO YOUR RESEARCH

There's plenty of information online about any game. Whether it's the right setup for your *FIFA* team or secret areas in *Ori* that offer useful power-ups, always ensure you do your research before, or even while you play.

PLAY THE TUTORIAL

We know, tutorials can be boring when you just want to dive straight into the game. But you can pick up useful tips from the tutorial, and learn some controls that might otherwise take you a while to discover for yourself. Plus, you sometimes get an Achievement or Trophy for finishing it!

PLAY TOUGH RIVALS

If a friend keeps beating you at a multiplayer game, rise to the challenge. Keep playing them. Study what they're doing well and use their own tactics to beat them.

BE PERSISTENT

It can be easy to give up, especially in puzzle games like *Stick it to the Man* or *The Witness*. But keep going! You could look for a solution online, but if you experiment with new ideas, you'll improve your play for later.

GET REST

If you're feeling tired, your reactions will suffer. Go to humanbenchmark.com and try the reaction test. If you're clocking slow reaction times, you need to take a break right away. Go relax or get some rest!

⚡ HUMAN BENCHMARK   DASHBOARD   GAMES   0   👤 Sign up

Click to start

When the red box turns green, click as quickly as you can.

Average | 0ms   Tries | 0 of 5

TRY NEW IDEAS

If you're really stuck, try a new tactic. Maybe try running new plays in *Madden NFL,* a new character in *Overwatch,* or a new weapon in *Mighty No. 9.* You could even get tips from your friends.

GO INTO OPTIONS

Some games will give you the option to change your camera view, sensitivity, or even the controls, depending on which character you're using. Go through all the options and tailor them to suit your preferences.

WATCH TOURNAMENTS

Watching the best gamers in action will give you fresh ideas on how to play. You can watch live games and tournaments on websites such as YouTube, where they're streamed for free.

💡 QUICK TRICKS

1 PUSH IN ANALOG STICKS
Sometimes analog sticks can end up "pushed out" during play, so just click them back in to make sure you have total control over your character.

2 WAIT FOR THE INSTALL
Some games will let you start playing before the install is complete. But wait for it to finish before you play, or you may end up waiting for the game to finish downloading.

3 SWITCH ON "GAME MODE"
Some TVs will have a "Game Mode" option in their settings. Switch this on to get the very best visuals.

4 KEEP THE SCREEN BRIGHT
Go to Options menu and change the brightness settings so you can see background details clearly.

HOW TO BECOME A BETTER GAMER

WHAT TO PRACTICE AND WHAT TO AVOID

CHECK YOUR BATTERY

Check your controller's battery level before you start playing. You don't want your batteries to die mid-Achievement attempt! And remember, if it dies in an online game, you can't pause . . .

DO

USE MUTE

Noisy players can be distracting when you're trying to beat a high score, but you can mute them. On Xbox One, choose the profile of a player and select Mute. On PS4, just create a solo party chat, which will mute others.

USE PRACTICE MODE

If the game you're playing has a practice or training mode—like *Street Fighter V* or *Overwatch*—use it. This gives you a chance to perfect all the special moves away from competitive play.

ASK FRIENDS FOR HELP

Sometimes your friends will have beaten certain levels or will know how to play against certain characters. In co-op games, get them to help you out by playing alongside you.

SHARE YOUR GLORY

When you do finally unlock that elusive Achievement or Trophy, share the moment with your friends. That way, other players that are trying to unlock the same thing can use your video or screenshot as a guide.

Did you know?

On Xbox One, you can see saved video clips from any player by looking up their profile from the Home screen. It's useful to see what good players are doing!

DON'T

GET MAD

Don't get angry if you keep losing or if you're really stuck on a certain level. Keep cool and analyze the situation. Stay calm, stay focused, and figure out what you need to do in order to progress in the game.

ZENYATTA

STREAM MUSIC OR TV

There are some people who will stream from apps while playing, but, if you want to be the best, it's not advisable. Not only does it slow down your broadband connection, it will also distract you.

NETFLIX

Something for everyone.
FAMILY FAVOURITES TO WATCH TOGETHER.

JOIN FREE FOR A MONTH

EAT WHILE PLAYING

This is bad for two reasons. First of all, it's distracting and ruins your focus on the game. Secondly, it makes your fingers greasy, causing the controller to slip and slide everywhere—which is a bad idea in a precision game like *Rocket League*.

Did you know?

Sony didn't add Trophies to its games until July 2008—almost two years after the PS3 was released in Japan and the US.

BLAME THE GAME

If you're really stuck on a tricky game like *Trials Fusion*, don't blame the game. Instead, ask yourself: "What could I do differently? Is there another way of tackling the problem?"

PLAY FOR TOO LONG

Even silly games like *Goat Simulator* can be too difficult if you're exhausted. Know when to call it quits. You can always play again the next day. You should take short breaks every hour.

QUICK TIPS & TRICKS

PLANTS VS. ZOMBIES GARDEN WARFARE 2

Every character has unique abilities that can be used to do more damage or help your team, such as Kernel Corn's Shuck Shot. Once you use it, the skill will have to recharge for a few seconds before you can use it again. Remember to check the bottom corner of the screen regularly, so you can use your skills as soon as they're ready to go again!

LEGO STAR WARS: THE FORCE AWAKENS

LEGO video games are great at taking an already amazing franchise and injecting it with some trademark LEGO humor, to give it a new twist. They've pulled it off again with this title that lets you relive the awesome *Force Awakens* movie.

TIPS & STRATEGY

BEGINNER
COLLECT THEM ALL

Don't ignore studs, because collecting them will allow you to unlock more cool stuff. Break the environment up to find more to collect.

MULTI-BUILDS

A new multi-build system lets you construct different things based on which direction you hold while building. If you pick the wrong option, simply smash it up and start again.

INTERMEDIATE
RUNNING RINGS

Always keep a lookout for purple rings when in a TIE fighter. Flying through them will begin a timed run.

THE DRIVER'S SEAT

Practice piloting the vehicles you find in the game's hubs. They'll help you get around faster and are more effective at destroying objects that could hide secrets.

ADVANCED
CROWD CONTROL

When your combat bar fills, try to get into a crowd so you can take out multiple enemies when you unleash your special move by pressing B or Circle.

SECRET HUNTER

Red Bricks and Minikits are hidden throughout the game. Check every corner and try every variation of multi-build just in case they hide a secret.

CHEATS & SECRETS

UNLOCK TEEDO

Head into the pause menu, select Enter Code, and then input the code CP6ETU to unlock Teedo.

A SECRET HOPE

In a small hut towards the top of the Jakku level, you can find a LEGO-style version of the original *Star Wars* poster.

TOP 3 Achievements & Trophies

☑ EASIEST ACHIEVEMENT
LITTLE SHORT FOR A STORMTROOPER?
Use a hat dispenser to put a Stormtrooper helmet on a small minifigure

A throwback to a classic *Star Wars* line, you can grab this Achievement in the Shield Room of Starkiller Base. Walk over to the hat dispenser with an Ewok and put Stormtrooper helmet on.

☻ FUNNIEST TROPHY
STORMTROOPER SYNDROME
Miss your target 10 times in a blaster battle

This Trophy makes fun of the Stormtroopers' infamously bad aim in the movies. Just make sure you totally miss ten times in a single battle.

☺ COOLEST ACHIEVEMENT
CHEWIE, WE'RE HOME
Play as Han Solo (Classic) and Chewbacca on the *Millennium Falcon*

You'll need the Classic Han Solo minifigure to make this reunion complete, which means tracking down the carbonite collectible and reviving him at D'Qar. Once the classic Han is unfrozen, get him on board the *Millennium Falcon* with Chewie and you're set!

BECOME A JEDI MASTER

29,700

5   1

1. COMBAT METER

Fully charging this meter will let you unleash your character's special ability. Try and hold off using it until you're facing a group of enemies to make it really count.

2. ENERGY SHIELDS

Some enemies will be protected by a force field, which will need deactivating before they can be defeated. Look out for generators and disable them to turn off the force field.

ANYTHING ELSE?
LET THE HATE FLOW THROUGH YOU

*Can use dark side Force powers
*Can accept First Order missions
*Can use First Order Terminals

R1

Kylo Ren (Unmasked)

Exit   Accept

UNLOCK KYLO

1 First things first, to get this Achievement you'll need to unlock one of the three Kylo Ren minifigures. The first should become available to use after you complete Chapter nine.

BUST UP TERMINALS

2 Now head over to the Starkiller Base Shield Room and use Kylo to destroy all the black and red terminals you see. There are three before the red barrier and two after it.

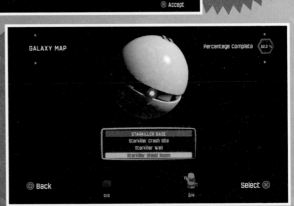

GALAXY MAP   Percentage Complete 82.2%

STARKILLER BASE
Starkiller Crash Site
Starkiller Wall
Starkiller Shield Room

Back   0/0   0/4   Select

3. ENEMY INDICATORS

When in combat, you'll be given a snapshot of all the different enemies in an area here. If there's still one left up here, chances are they're hiding somewhere.

4. TARGET ACQUIRED

Holding the fire button lets you aim your weapon precisely. Think tactically about which enemies you want to take out first and focus your fire (or Force powers) on them.

THE EXPERT SAYS . . .

ZACH DRAPALA
(GHOSTROBO)

Known for:

Streaming and commentating at youtube.com/ GhostRobo

The main keys to succeeding in LEGO *Star Wars: The Force Awakens* are exploration and multi-builds. Try and explore the whole map, even areas that seem out of sight, and try to keep your eyes peeled for multi-builds. Beating the levels in the game is a lot more fun and involved because of this awesome new puzzle mechanic. Make sure you try out all of the multi-build options available if you want success . . . and studs!

USE RED BRICKS

3 Red bricks can really come in handy here, especially the brick "Destroy on Contact." With this setting enabled, you can just walk into the terminals to break them apart.

FRIENDLY FIRE

4 Be careful in the shoot-out on the upper level—it has to be you who breaks the computers. If another character destroys a terminal, you'll have to start again.

MINECRAFT

Craft items, mine for resources, and then combine them to build mighty towers, cool houses, epic castles, or whatever else you want! Even better, you can also explore *Minecraft*'s huge procedurally generated worlds with friends.

TIPS & STRATEGY

BEGINNER
LIGHT IT UP

Make sure any structure you build is well lit with torches to stop enemies spawning and messing it all up!

INFINITE WATER

Dig a three-by-one trench and place water at either end. As long as you take water only from the middle block, you've got an infinite water source.

INTERMEDIATE
MAKE YOUR BED

If you're entering an area that you think could be dangerous, craft a bed and sleep in it. This will now be set as your new spawn point. Leave some resources behind just in case!

COOLING OFF

It's worth taking a few snowballs with you into The Nether as they can do damage to the Blaze mobs you'll fight.

ADVANCED
ENCHANTING

Collect four obsidian blocks, two diamonds, and one book to build an enchanting table. You can then enchant items to make them more powerful.

MAKE A BREW

Potions can give you an edge in tougher fights. Craft a brewing stand and mix up Potions of Regeneration, Night Vision, and Healing before fighting the Ender Dragon, to increase your chances of winning.

CHEATS & SECRETS

COOL PAINTINGS

Some of the paintings you can decorate with reference classic video games, such as *Donkey Kong*.

THE FAST APPROACH

Hit the bottom block of sand or gravel and quickly place a torch in its place. It will destroy every block in the stack.

TOP 4 Achievements & Trophies

☑ EASIEST ACHIEVEMENT
TAKING INVENTORY
Open your inventory

It would be a bigger challenge to play *Minecraft* without completing this challenge. All you have to do is bring up your inventory by pressing Y on Xbox, or Triangle on PlayStation. It's that simple.

↔ TOUGHEST ACHIEVEMENT
THE END
Kill the Enderdragon

Before taking on *Minecraft*'s toughest mob, make sure you've got strong, enchanted weapons and armor, some healing items, and a Potion of Night Vision to help you spot the dragon easily.

☻ COOLEST TROPHY
SNIPER DUEL
Kill a skeleton with an arrow from more than 50 meters

There's a clever way to unlock this Achievement or Trophy. Rather than trying to stand 50 meters away on the ground, build 50 blocks into the sky, near a skeleton. Then take aim from the top of the pillar to complete the challenge.

☺ FUNNIEST TROPHY
TRAMPOLINE
Bounce 30 blocks upward off a Slime Block

Lay down a bed of slime blocks that's a big enough target to hit and then build the tallest diving board ever seen! Then all you need to do is walk off to get the huge bounce you need.

LION TAMER
TAME AN OCELOT

PLAY TUTORIAL

1 Play through the tutorial until you can pass through the opening in the wall. Head to the small farm area with animals in pens.

GRAB THE FISH

2 There's a chest in the middle of this area. Grab the raw fish from the chest, as this is what you'll need to tame the ocelot.

FREE THE OCELOT

3 Open the pen or break the fence so the ocelot runs free. Equip the raw fish, crouch down, and wait until the ocelot feels less scared.

OCELOT TAMED

4 The ocelot will walk toward you. When it gets close, use the raw fish on the ocelot and a flurry of hearts will appear. You've tamed the ocelot!

BODY GUARD
CREATE AN IRON GOLEM

GATHER IRON

1 Head to the enchantment area. Take the stone pickax and head toward the beacon area to start mining iron. Gather four blocks of iron to create the iron golem, which will fight off nearby monsters.

START BUILDING

2 Now you need to build the arms. Build two iron blocks, just like in the screenshot on the right. Next, add a block on each side of the top iron block, so that it resembles a "T" shape.

MUSIC TO MY EARS
PLAY A MUSIC DISK IN A JUKEBOX

1. TUTORIAL AREA

You can unlock "Music to my Ears" in the starting tutorial area, because you can find the necessary Jukebox and Music Discs here.

2. GRAB JUKEBOX

When you complete the first area and walk up the stone steps, you find a chest straight ahead. This contains the Jukebox and Music Discs.

3. PLAY THE MUSIC

Put the Jukebox on the ground. Now open your inventory and use any of the Music Discs you picked up in the Jukebox. Challenge complete.

PUMPKIN HEAD

3 Once you've built the iron blocks for the body, you need to place a pumpkin block on top, as the head. You can get your hands on a pumpkin from the tutorial farm area.

GOLEM COMPLETE

4 When complete, your iron golem will start walking around. You'll also get a notification to confirm the Achievement or Trophy is unlocked.

EASIEST ☑
ACHIEVEMENTS
& TROPHIES
EVER

THESE CHALLENGES ARE A PUSHOVER . . .

ORI AND THE BLIND FOREST

MARKING THE WAY

Restore your first Map Stone

To unlock this Achievement, you simply have to explore the Sunken Glades. As you advance through the level, you'll find the Map Stone Fragment, and soon after you'll find the Map Stone itself—press X to restore it.

20

19

NEED FOR SPEED RIVALS
FIRST NATIONAL
Bank your first score

You don't have to go out of your way to complete this challenge. The beginning of *Rivals*' career mode will put you in a racer tutorial. "First National" will unlock as soon as it's complete. Unmissable and incredibly easy.

FIFA 16
I AM THE BOSS
Substitute your star player (the highest rated player on your team) in a game

During any game, all you have to do is substitute the player with the highest rating on your team. You can even do this during the closing stages of an offline exhibition game if you don't want to risk a loss that might harm your online win record.

18

DC UNIVERSE ONLINE
PLATINUM PACE
Earn a Platinum medal in any race

17

1 FIND A RACE
There are lots of races dotted around Gotham and Metropolis. The ones near the hideouts are generally easier.

2 NOW RACE
Follow the rings to complete the race. Don't try and cut corners or take big risks, as you have time on your side.

3 AND DONE!
Races are usually between 60 seconds and three minutes, so restart if you fail. Soon you'll ace this easy Trophy.

16

WWE 2K16
GENTLEMAN IN THE RING
Push opponent into the ropes during chain wrestling to perform a clean break

You can only get into a chain wrestling lock-up near the start of a match, when both wrestlers are still fresh. When you lock up, push your opponent to the ropes and *ignore* the on-screen prompt to initiate a clean break.

PRO EVOLUTION SOCCER 2016
ONLINE DEBUTANT
Awarded for completing your debut match in [Online]

The only criteria that needs to be satisfied here is that you complete your first online match in *Pro Evolution Soccer 2016*. You don't even need to win it! Just stick around until the match is finished to unlock the Achievement or Trophy.

15

14

TRANSFORMERS: DEVASTATION
PEDAL TO THE METAL
Used Focus 100 times

If you want to master *Transformers: Devastation*, this is the challenge to focus on—literally. When you dodge an attack at the last possible moment, you'll activate Focus, which slows down time. Doing this 100 times sounds like a lot but it's really not—you will easily unlock this just by playing the first few levels.

13 RATCHET & CLANK
KALEBO THUNDER

Complete the hoverboard Gold Cup on Kalebo in under 2:05

You have a huge margin for error with this Trophy, and you can unlock shortcuts, too—activate the three rings to do so. If you have five gold bolts, you can even buy a cheat in the Extras menu to make the game slower, making this Trophy even easier.

12

GODZILLA
RECURRING NIGHTMARE
Go ashore for the first time in God of Destruction mode

This isn't something you have to manually do in the game itself. Enter God of Destruction mode and you'll see the option to "Go ashore." This is actually related to the story mode in the game—simply select it and you'll unlock the Trophy.

FORZA HORIZON 2
WELCOME TO HORIZON EUROPE
Arrive at the Horizon Festival

This will likely be the first Achievement you unlock in *Forza Horizon 2*. When you start the game, you'll be driving a Lamborghini Huracan. Just follow the directions and you'll soon arrive at the Horizon Festival. The Achievement unlocks when the cutscene plays.

11

10 OVERWATCH
THE CAR WASH
Hit an enemy with 7 beams simultaneously as Symmetra

1. NUMBANI MAP
This Achievement or Trophy is much easier than it first seems. The trick is to try this on the Numbani map when playing on defense. This is because there's this chokepoint by the payload.

2. SET UP TURRETS
During the setup phase, put your turrets around this doorway. Don't worry about them being too far apart. Make sure attackers can't see them, though, until they've stepped through.

HAVE MERCY
might be worth keeping rcy on standby. There's a ance the team will attack om the main "lane" of the ap, in which case you'll need stay alive until they retreat.

4. AND WAIT . . .
Wait for an enemy to stumble through and get hit by the six turrets. Your gun is the seventh beam you need for this Achievement or Trophy.

9

GHOSTBUSTERS
"A" IS FOR APPARITION
Get an A ranking on a single level
This is easier than you might think. As you play through any level of *Ghostbusters*, destroy everything while keeping your multiplier going. Don't worry if you drop the combo. Just keep destroying everything for an easy "A" rank in any early level.

INJUSTICE: GODS AMONG US
FINISHED
Win a match with the super move of any character
During *Injustice*, you'll fill up super move bars by performing moves, attacking, taking damage, and more. When you have three bars, you can use your super move by pressing L2 and R2 on PS4, or RT and LT on Xbox One. If this move finishes off your opponent, the Trophy or Achievement will pop.

8

7 PROJECT CARS

READY TO POUNCE

Have a reaction time of less than 0.2 secs off the starting grid

The easiest way to unlock this Achievement or Trophy is to ensure you use automatic gearing and hit the throttle as soon as the light turns green. 0.2 seconds might not seem like much time, but keep trying and you'll get it!

6 DIRT RALLY

HOW YOU LIKE ME NOW?

Change your Livery

Your first task in *Dirt Rally* is to buy a car, which unlocks an Achievement or Trophy. Now all you have to do is press LB or RB (L1 or R1 if you're on PlayStation) and you'll unlock a second Achievement or Trophy—this time for changing your livery. It's very easy to do, but also very easy to miss!

5 NBA 2K16

RUN 'N' GUN

Make a three-pointer off of a fast break

1 GRAB THE BALL
The easiest way to do this is by either grabbing a rebound off your opponent's missed shot or stealing the ball.

2 QUICKLY SHOOT
Now race up the court (so it counts as a "fast break") and take the three-pointer with a good shooter on your team.

3 AND DONE
If the three-pointer goes in, you'll receive a notification that you've unlocked the Achievement or Trophy.

4 WORLD OF TANKS
VICTORY
Survive, and win a battle. MP only

You will earn this without even trying, if you play *World of Tanks* enough. However there's a smart way to speed up the process and make it much easier. Don't fight! Either hang back or pick artillery, so you're excused from the frontline action. Just remember—you have to be in multiplayer to unlock this one.

6 QUICK-FIRE ACHIEVEMENTS AND TROPHIES

NHL 16
NOT MY GATORADE!
Knock off the opposing goalie's Gatorade bottle from the net

Play a two-player game and get the second player to remove his or her goalie. Now go and score.

NARUTO SHIPPUDEN: ULTIMATE NINJA STORM 4
A CHAIN OF BATTLES
Complete The Creation Chapter

Just beat the first two missions in the game to complete this challenge.

FIGHTER WITHIN
COMBO HARVESTER
Perform 10 combos

You'll likely earn this in your first match just by fighting normally. Simply plug in and play and the Trophy or Achievement will pop.

SKYLANDERS SUPERCHARGERS
HORN HONKER
Honk your first vehicle horn

Just click in the left analog stick and you'll honk your vehicle's horn.

PLANTS VS. ZOMBIES GARDEN WARFARE 2
STAR CRAZY
Spend your first star

As soon as you earn your first star, spend it. It really is as easy as that!

ONE PIECE: BURNING BLOOD
PARAMOUNT WAR BEGINS!
Play Paramount War

Just begin any *Paramount War* chapter and this Trophy or Achievement will unlock.

CHECK GAMERSCORE VALUE

Achievements with lower Gamerscores tend to be the ones that are easy to unlock. Scroll through the list and target those.

CHECK TROPHY COLOR

The more valuable a Trophy is, the harder they are to unlock. So bronze Trophies are the easiest and quickest to unlock.

CHEATS & SECRETS

3

TONY HAWK'S PRO SKATER 5

NUMERO UNO

Earn a Stat Point by completing a mission at Pro Level

This challenge sounds scarier than it is. All you need to do is earn two stars in any mission available—it doesn't have to be a Pro mission. Pick Halycon High and you'll almost unlock this by mistake, as the requirement for Pro Level completion is incredibly generous.

2

OVERCOOKED

OVERCOOKED

Extinguish a burning kitchen

All you need to do is let your kitchen catch fire and then put the fire out to unlock this Trophy or Achievement. And you can do it on the very first level. Chop an onion or tomato and throw it into a pot. Leave it cooking and eventually it will catch fire. Grab the fire extinguisher and put the fire out. Easy!

1

BACK TO THE FUTURE: THE GAME

BACK IN TIME

Time travel to rescue Doc

During the first episode, "It's About Time," you'll move to a back alley with the DeLorean after being in Edna's apartment. Use the Time Circuit Switch, the Time Circuit Keypad, or talk to George and that's it. Job done!

sometimes you gotta go out on a limb for this one, ya boys, right? I wish Biff told had...

START ON EASY

Sometimes you can complete games on Easy mode and then take your items, stats, and more through to your next playthrough. This makes high difficulty levels much easier.

GAMER INTERVIEW

CASINO83
📢 Known for:
Having one of the highest Gamerscore totals in the world

GERMAN GAMER CASINO83 IS CLOSING IN ON A 1,000,000 GAMERSCORE. THIS IS HOW HE GOT THERE . . .

When did you decide to start chasing the highest Gamerscore possible?
I decided to get a high Gamerscore when I unlocked my first Achievement in *Need For Speed: Most Wanted* on the Xbox 360, back in November 2005.

What games have been the hardest for you for unlocking Achievements?
I don't like games that focus on online multiplayer Achievements, because most of them are only unlockable for a short space of time. After a few years, the multiplayer servers are shut down and online multiplayer Achievements become unobtainable.

Which games have been your favorite for Achievements?
Since the Xbox One "ID@Xbox" program started and every game had their minimum Gamerscore raised to 1000G, I've preferred to play "ID@ Xbox" games to unlock Achievements. The games tend to be quite simple!

ARCADE GAME SERIES™

Galaga™

Casino83 plays all sorts of games for Achievements, like *Galaga*, *Scrabble*, and *Barbie and Her Sisters Puppy Rescue*.

"GETTING A HIGH GAMERSCORE IS ABOUT TIME."

Using a guide, it's possible to nab all the Achievements in games like *Clockwork Tales* without too much fuss.

Why is your Gamerscore so high?
Getting a high Gamerscore is all about time. The skill comes naturally. You get better and better if you just put time into it.

Have there been games you didn't want to play, but after playing them for Achievements, you liked them?
Oh yeah, a few of them I never would've played if not for Achievements. Point-and-click games like *Clockwork Tales: Of Glass and Ink*, for example. I wouldn't have played them until I realized that they are quite simple, and easy with a guide.

What do other players say about your Gamerscore?
Most games are respectful and friendly since the Xbox One update. It allows players to Like, Share, and Comment on Achievements being unlocked, gaming clips being saved, and screenshots being taken.

Could you catch Stallion83, the record holder for the highest number of Achievements?
No, and I don't want to catch anyone. I'm proud to be in the top 20 of Gamerscore hunters worldwide.

What advice would you give to someone who wants to get a high Gamerscore, like you?
Follow other people that have a high Gamerscore and watch what they play. Watch guides or walkthroughs on YouTube. Then, getting a high Gamerscore is down to time.

NO MAN'S SKY

No Man's Sky offers a vast galaxy of different worlds to explore as you travel to the center of the universe. Over 18 quintillion planets are made using procedural generation, meaning every one is unique—and totally random.

TIPS & STRATEGY

BEGINNER ◄

FOLLOW THE ATLAS PATH

If you want to see all the strangest things during your adventure in the *No Man's Sky* universe, stay on the Atlas Path to learn more about the world you're exploring.

KEEP YOUR ATLAS STONES

Even though Atlas stones are worth a lot of money, you should keep hold of them. If you collect ten stones they can be used for something very cool later in the game.

INTERMEDIATE ◄◄

SAVE YOUR FUEL

Taking off uses a lot of fuel in your Launch Thrusters, but it costs nothing if you use a landing pad. Keep an eye out for them to save the Plutonium in your inventory.

BUY LOW, SELL HIGH

Always look out for gold stars positioned next to items in the Galactic Trade Network. These are worth twice as much. Buy them cheap from other traders and you can make money fast at space stations.

ADVANCED ◄◄◄

QUICK SHIP UPGRADES

When you find a crashed ship, it will always have an extra slot for items compared to yours. If you keep replacing your ship with these and fixing them, you will have much more room for upgrades later.

CHEATS & SECRETS

QUICK MOVEMENT

Use run and then hit melee and jetpack really close together to enjoy a speedy leap forward.

ENTER THE ORE

On hostile worlds, try mining a hole in the ore you want and standing inside. The Sentinels will leave you alone.

↔ TOUGHEST TROPHY
GALAPAGOS
Attain "Encyclopedia" status in Uploaded Discoveries

Unlock this Trophy by finding all the records on ten different planets. That means scanning and uploading info on all the living creatures on ten different worlds. Speed up the process by finding planets with only a few creatures.

💎 RAREST TROPHY
TOTAL PERSPECTIVE VORTEX
Platinum

No Man's Sky doesn't tell you what it takes to unlock this one, but we can. You actually need to unlock all the other Trophies in the game. It's also a reference to the cult science fiction series *The Hitchhikers' Guide to the Galaxy*.

☑ EASIEST TROPHY
CONTACT
Attain 'Known' status in Alien Colonist Encounters

All you need to do to gain this Trophy is meet a few aliens. Just keep introducing yourself to all the different life forms you find in buildings and this will pop up pretty quickly on your journey.

🎮 COOLEST TROPHY
CITIZEN OF THE GALAXY
Attain "Babelfish" status in Words Collected

This is all about learning alien words. Keep interacting with Monoliths, Knowledge Stones, and ancient ruins, and their jumbled text will begin to turn into words that you can decipher. This makes it much easier to communicate.

RATCHET & CLANK

PlayStation legends Ratchet and Clank return in this epic reboot of the action platformer series. Expect tons of crazy weapons, some amazing graphics, and plenty of side-splitting jokes to accompany the action.

TIPS & STRATEGY

BEGINNER
CRATE SMASHER

Be on the lookout for crates and be sure to smash them when you see them. You'll get bolts that you can use to buy ammo, health, and weapons.

CARD COLLECTOR

Keep an eye on your stock of collectible cards. If you get five duplicates, you can trade them in for a new card.

INTERMEDIATE
GET MORE XP

Always use weapons instead of your wrench when possible. Doing so will gain you more XP to help you level up that specific weapon, as well as general XP for your character.

SET THE BEAT

The Proton Drum is a great weapon for dealing with crowds of enemies, as it damages anyone that is close to you when you use it.

ADVANCED
KEEP SWITCHING

Become an expert with every weapon by swapping regularly. This means you will level up every weapon, rather than ending up with tons of weak, useless ones.

GETTING 100%

Don't try to find every collectible during your first playthrough. You need to come back later with the new abilities you've unlocked.

CHEATS & SECRETS

CHEAT MODE

Once you have defeated Drek, head into the Goodies menu and you can turn on cheats. These include Big Head mode and invincibility.

THE SILVER SCREEN

Have you watched the *Ratchet & Clank* movie? If so, you might have noticed that clips from the movie are used as cutscenes in the game.

TOP 4 Trophies

✅ EASIEST TROPHY
THAT SINKING FEELING
Knock a Constructobot into the quicksand on "Aridia"

Use your wrench to knock your enemy into quicksand. Be careful, though—you can only hit these robots a few times before they explode.

🕵 SECRET TROPHY
WHEN SHEEP FLY
Sheepinate a Blarg Helicopter Commander

Once you reach Kalebo III near the end of the game, grab the Sheepinator weapon from the kiosk. Blast the next helicopter you see with the gun until it becomes a sheep.

😀 WEIRDEST TROPHY
I HATE LAMP
Break every single lamp in Aleero City

Exactly why Ratchet needs to smash up streetlights, we'll never know. Still, there are 17 in total to break if you want this Trophy, so do a lap around the city and destroy every one you see.

↔ HARDEST TROPHY
CHA-CHING!
Reach the maximum bolt multiplier in Challenge Mode

Taking a single hit while building your multiplier will cancel it. So find a simple checkpoint, take out a few enemies, and quit to the main menu. Your multiplier will still be intact when you reload, so just keep doing this.

QUICK TIPS & TRICKS

TEENAGE MUTANT NINJA TURTLES: MUTANTS IN MANHATTAN

You don't have to run to get around the city. The Turtles can grind along the walls of buildings, or glide using these parachutes, to get around without taking to the streets. This is great when you want to get a better view of what's going on below. And if you combine these skills to travel for one mile without touching the ground, you'll even unlock a Trophy or Achievement!

PLANTS vs. ZOMBIES GARDEN WARFARE 2

The ongoing battle between the plants and zombies continues in this awesome multiplayer shooter. Teamwork and strategy are just as important as your shooting skills when you take on the enemy team!

TIPS & STRATEGY

BEGINNER
AN EASY PICK

IIf you're new to the game, try picking Super Brainz or Kernel Corn. They are good all-arounders, which means they are pretty simple to play.

PLAY THE OBJECTIVE

Always focus on the objective of the match type you are playing. Shooting down loads of enemies is pointless, if it's not part of your objective.

INTERMEDIATE
CHECK THE BOARD

Make sure to check the Quest Board regularly and to pick the quests that match the game modes and characters you like to play.

NEXT LEVEL

Keep playing as a character to level them up and unlock new abilities. This will make them more powerful in battle.

ADVANCED
BALANCE THE TEAM

Get good enough to play as any character and you can always give the team what it needs. No healer? You can pick the Sunflower and fix that right away.

GET PROMOTED

When a character reaches level 10, head into the stats room and you can choose to promote them. This sets them back to level 1 and earns you 20,000 coins in the process.

CHEATS & SECRETS

GOLDEN GNOMES

There are 54 Golden Gnomes hidden throughout *Plants vs. Zombies Garden Warfare 2*, so keep your eyes peeled!

SECRET TREASURE

In the Crazy Target area, look for a flimsy wood panel. When you find it, shoot it down and you will find a treasure room on the other side.

TOP 3 Achievements & Trophies

😊 FUNNIEST ACHIEVEMENT
PRANCE VS. SAMBA
Gesture immediately after vanquishing an enemy

Your first hour or two of *Garden Warfare 2* can be frustrating if players with more experience keep beating you. But once you get the hang of a character or map you'll start to rack up points. So why not celebrate a win with a little boogie?

😎 COOLEST TROPHY
SIMPLY SUPER
As Super Brainz, vanquish 25 Plants with Heroic Fists, and 25 Plants with the Heroic Beam

Use your Heroic Beam on any enemies in the distance. If they dare to get up close, rush them to use Super Brainz powerful melee Heroic Fists attack—one of the most fun and coolest looking attacks in the game. Keep plugging away and eventually the Trophy will pop.

↔ TOUGHEST ACHIEVEMENT
INSANITY
Complete an Ops game on CRRRRRAAAZY Mode

A round of Ops can be tough at the best of times, but crank up the difficulty to the highest setting (it's called "CRRRRRAAAZY" for a reason, you know) and you're in for a real battle. You can swap between up to three characters on your own, but you're better off doing this one as a team.

KNOW YOUR ICONS

THE HEALTH ICON

her than your ammo,
e most important thing to
eep an eye on is your health.
he heart icon has a number
eside it, which decreases
hen you take a hit.

2. THE XP METER

Everything you
do in each match—
beating other
players, completing
objectives, and so
on—will gain you XP.
The more XP you
gain, the more the
bar fills, and each
time it does you will
grow a little stronger.

3. THE AMMUNITION COUNTER

Each character in
Garden Warfare 2
has a specific
weapon, with a
standard number
of shots it can take
before it needs
loading again.

RGBY
VANQUISH GNOMUS, THE GNOME KING!

IGNORE THE MINIONS

1 Gnomus loves
to send out plenty
of gnome minions to
slow you down. Don't
pay much attention to
them, because each
time he takes a big
chunk of damage, he
disappears and
so do his minions.

DEFEAT THE IMPOSTERS

2 Gnomus sends
out an impostor
king to fight you
after every five
waves. These will
be red, green, blue
and yellow. You
need to fight each
one to reach
Gnomus himself.

4. THE SPECIAL ABILITIES BAR

Each zombie or plant has a set of special abilities that can be activated at the press of a single button (they'll need to recharge after every use, though).

7 Pea Cannon

THE EXPERT SAYS...

ZACK SCOTT

Known for: His PvZGW2 videos on YouTube

"I got into YouTube making comedy videos of cats and spiders. Eventually I followed my gaming passion and my ZackScottGames channel took off from there.

"I've always loved the *Plants vs. Zombies* games, and I was an avid player of the first *Garden Warfare*. *Garden Warfare 2* improved on everything awesome about the first, so I just had to play it!

"*Garden Warfare 2* is a team-based game, so you'll do well if your team does well. Try your best to help your team, and as always, practice makes perfect!"

FIGHT HIS HENCHMAN

3 When Gnomus is down to a quarter of his health, he vanishes again and sends in two giant enemies for you to fight. Use your Furball Frenzy/Epic Mega Blast to take them down quickly.

GNOMUS IS YOURS

4 When the two henchman are defeated, Gnomus will try to beat you himself. Once again, rely on your specials such as Epic Mega Blast to take him down quickly.

ROCKET LEAGUE

Rocket League puts you in control of rocket-powered cars, and lets you loose in an arena with two goals and a gigantic ball in a crazy version of soccer. It's just awesome fun for beginners, but becomes a real game of skill.

TIPS & STRATEGY

BEGINNER
STOP COUNTERS

If everyone rushes forward to score, you're going to concede goals. One players should always be hanging back to prevent counterattacks.

FUEL UP

Always drive over boost pads as you move around the arena so you've got some fuel in the tank when you need it.

INTERMEDIATE
COMMUNICATE

Talk to your friends when you are playing together. Make sure you don't go for the same ball, and can position yourselves to pick up on each other's passes.

EMERGENCY BOOST

If your boost bar is empty, front-flipping is an alternative way of getting a quick little speed boost.

ADVANCED
RUN INTERFERENCE

If there's someone playing the role of goalkeeper for the other team, try crashing into them when one of your teammates is about to shoot.

LEARN TO FLY

Using your boost to fly into the air by pointing your car's nose upwards is one of *Rocket League*'s hardest skills. But it is also one of its most valuable, as it allows you to get to high balls first.

CHEATS & SECRETS

TIP OF THE HAT

Two of the cars in *Rocket League* are from its predecessor, *Super Acrobatic Rocket-Powered Battle Cars.*

GOING OLD-SCHOOL

On the main menu, enter the Konami Code (Up, Up, Down, Down, Left, Right, Left, Right, B, A, Start) to see the startup screen for *SARPBC.*

⊘ COOLEST ACHIEVEMENT
SKY HIGH
Score an Aerial Goal

There's no greater feeling in *Rocket League* than soaring through the sky to bag an aerial goal. Hang around the halfway line and wait for the right cross before using your boost to go flying in.

✓ EASIEST ACHIEVEMENT
GREASE MONKEY
Customize every slot on a single Battle-Car

Once you've unlocked a few items, simply head into the customization screen to tweak your wheels, boost, antenna, decals, and toppers. It's as easy as that.

🏆 SECRET TROPHY
BATTLE-CAR COLLECTOR
Unlock all Battle-Cars

This isn't a secret Trophy as such, but there is a secret behind getting it. You'll unlock cars for playing matches, but what the game doesn't tell you is that the last car won't unlock until you win one game with every other car in the roster.

THE EXPERT SAYS . . .

PAUL WALKER-EMIG
Games writer

One of the tougher Trophies that I grabbed on my way to getting the Platinum requires you to get six goals in one match. If you're struggling, get some friends to join you and let you score!

HOW TO MASTER LOCAL MULTIPLAYER

GET ALL THOSE TROPHIES & ACHIEVEMENTS, WITH OR WITHOUT YOUR FRIENDS

Local multiplayer looked like a thing of the past when online multiplayer became the "in" thing at the start of this console generation. Fortunately, game developers soon realized that a lot of players still enjoy gaming with their friends in the same room!

There are a lot of titles that require you to play with friends to get Achievements . . . or so they'd like you to think! You can actually "boost" a lot of these rewards by yourself. All you need are two controllers, some fast fingers, and a bit of concentration.

Of course, if you just want to face off against your friends—or team up with them to beat a game together—you need to know how to play like a pro. Here's our guide to being awesome at local multiplayer titles, and getting the best Trophies and Achievements.

6 ESSENTIAL TIPS
Improve your multiplayer skills with these hints

KNOW YOUR GOALS

1 A lot of multiplayer Achievements will require you to get to certain levels or pull off a certain amount of moves to unlock the reward. If you and your friend are both trying to, say, "drive 500km" in *Rocket League*, you need to *never* stop driving in the arena. Read every Trophy and Achievement list before playing.

DON'T BE AFRAID OF LOSING

2 Knowing your limits in co-op modes is essential to success. If you and a buddy pick up *Resogun* and expect to complete all of the Experienced difficulty levels on the first go, you'll be disappointed. Don't worry though— when you go down, focus on getting back in and helping your friend!

KEEP COUNT OF WHAT YOU'RE DOING

3 There are games out there that need you to really grind for Trophies. Take *TowerFall Ascension*—a perfect game for you and up to three friends to play together. But even for a Bronze trophy, you'll have to play 5,000 rounds of Versus mode. Keep a tally—it'll help.

KNOW WHEN'S BEST TO PLAY

4 Some games have time-specific challenges to complete, and you won't want to miss them. In *Rayman Legends*, there's a reward for collecting 1,000,000 lums. Completing Daily and Weekly challenges is the key to reaching this number, so check back with friends regularly so you know when they reset.

TAKE ADVANTAGE OF CO-OP

5 If you need to tackle a long game, ask a friend to do it with you—it will be a lot more fun, and much faster! If you're playing the LEGO games in co-op, for example, a lot of the puzzles are far easier to solve with help. Also, the game doesn't stack difficulty, so combat becomes a bit more straightforward.

DON'T BE AFRAID TO USE A GUIDE

6 Sometimes you get stuck, and to find all those pesky secrets, you just need to get some help. Take *Never Alone*, for example—a great game, in which friends can help each other find secrets. Some of them are very tricky, so it's best if one of you looks up solutions and guides the other!

GUACAMELEE! A PERFECT GAME FOR FOUR FRIENDS

1. STRENGTH IN NUMBERS

When playing alone, you'll respawn at a save point if you're killed. In co-op, you just hover around your friends as a countdown ticks away, and then it's *much* easier to get back into the action.

2. PLATFORM PERFECTION

Take it in turns to tackle tricky platforming bits. If just one of you gets to the next area, everyone else warps there, making some of the hardest parts of the game very simple.

3. DRESS FOR SUCCESS

Different outfits give you different rewards, so mix and match with your friends to take advantage. Give the player that's better at combat the outfit that does more damage, for example.

YOU CAN BE COMPETITIVE IN RAYMAN LEGENDS

Compete with your friends in these creative ways

PLAY KUNG FOOT AGAINST EACH OTHER

1 *Rayman Legends* is about more than just running, jumping, collecting—there's also Kung Foot. Use your attacks to charge up and fire soccer balls. Try to get them past other players and score.

BEAT EACH OTHER'S TIMES

2 There are Daily and Weekly challenges in the game that feature leaderboards. There are "Extreme" ones for more seasoned players, and simple ones for friendly competition. Beat a score 50 times and you'll get a reward, too.

GO LUM CRAZY!

3 Try not to steal each others lums. If you get a pink one and then grab all the others in the sequence, you'll get double the score! However, if a friend jumps in and breaks the chain, you both lose out. So, make sure you grab them fast.

QUICK TIPS

4. COMBO CRAZY!

In battles, one character can pick up enemies to fling them at the other—use this to your advantage and don't even give your foes the opportunity to get up and attack!

EXAMINE EVERYTHING YOU SEE

You can make short work of big areas working in a team. Walk up to and "examine" *everything*.

LEAVE NO ENEMY STANDING

Enemies go down more quickly when you concentrate fire on them—work with friends to take everything down.

DON'T ALWAYS FOLLOW THE MAP

If the game wants you to go down one route, always look for other areas to explore. That's where secrets live!

03:00.983

1 pohapatu
2 Shogun
3 BlueBadger
4 katomariEU
5 ShiftySamurai
6 AN8A
7 DJ2witchy
Makereb

TRY HARDER MODES FIRST

Many games "stack" rewards so if you finish them on Hard, you get all the other Achievements or Trophies, too!

Did you know?

Not all Achievements or Trophies unlock for two players at once. Always research before bringing a friend in to help!

BE CREATIVE

A lot of rewards are handed out for creative plays or problem-solving. Always take advantage of the tools that the game gives you.

COMPLETE LEGO STAR WARS: THE FORCE AWAKENS WITH YOUR FRIENDS You don't have to fly solo

COMPLETE THE STORY

1 It's totally possible to get the Platinum or 1000G by playing LEGO *Star Wars: The Force Awakens* with your friends. Your best plan is to start off by completing the 12 story mode missions. Ignore the collectibles for now.

REPEAT STORY MODE IN FREE PLAY

2 Once you've finished the game, you can jump back in and use the right characters to unlock certain areas. You couldn't do this in the main game because they weren't unlocked yet, but now everything should be open to you!

GET ALL THE GOLD BRICKS

3 You should have 36 Gold Bricks by this point. You need to get 24 more if you want to unlock the rest of the game. If you're running short, enter the various hubworlds and look around there. Otherwise, jump into the New Star Wars adventure levels.

COMPLETE NEW STAR WARS ADVENTURE LEVELS

4 You'll need 60 Gold Bricks to unlock these missions. As in Step 1, just focus on getting through the missions before you try to collect everything. That way, when you jump back in for Step 5, you'll have a much easier time.

REPLAY NEW STAR WARS ADVENTURES IN FREE PLAY

5 As in Step 2, go back through all the levels with any characters that you want and unlock all the other areas you couldn't get to before. With a friend by your side, this mode becomes simple, so you can grab everything easily.

CLEAN UP

6 You *should* have everything in the game at this point, but if you don't, take a look at what specific tasks you need to complete. Go back in there and get it done. It really shouldn't take too long—then you can enjoy your Platinum or 1000 Gamerscore!

HOW TO COMPLETE LITTLEBIGPLANET3

LittleBigPlanet 3 is another game you can complete with your friends—well, up to three of them, in fact. But it's not an easy game: if you want to get the Platinum Trophy, you're going to have to work together and learn what each character can do.

ODDSOCK

Wall-jumping is a piece of cake to OddSock. He's the fastest and most agile of the new characters in the game. Make sure that when you're speeding through the levels with him, you take time to climb every wall: hidden items are absolutely *everywhere*.

SWOOP

If you can see a platform or item just out of reach, don't worry—Swoop will be able to help you. Swoop can fly to pretty much anywhere, making him the best item-snatching character. Make sure you revisit levels with him once you've unlocked him.

TOGGLE

When Toggle is big he becomes very strong, but when he's little he can fit where other characters can't. So, make sure you use his forms together. Shifting from big to small and using his height and weight to reach tricky places is what this guy's good for!

SACKBOY

Just because there are new characters doesn't mean that you should forget about the old one! Sackboy is more versatile than all of the others, so remember to select him and show him some love every now and then.

TOP5
REASONS LOCAL MULTIPLAYER GAMES RULE

1 EASIER GAMES

With a friend or three in the same room, a lot of games not only get a lot more fun, but they get a lot easier, too!

2 GREAT PRACTICE

Real players are often tougher opponents that the computer-controller characters. Practice against friends to improve your skills.

3 HAVING FUN

What's better than laughing with your friends online? Having them in the same room as you, and having an awesome time playing on the same screen—that's what!

4 CO-OP COMMUNICATION

If you're playing on a team with your friends, it's much easier to talk to them about strategies when they're sitting right next to you rather than communicating through a headset.

5 LEARN FROM FRIENDS

Don't feel bad if your friends are better than you at a game. Just watch them, learn what they do, and practice until you can beat them!

STAR WARS BATTLEFRONT

This is the *Star Wars* game you've always wanted. From piloting X-wings, to taking on Darth Vader in lightsaber duels, this online multiplayer shooter lets you relive the greatest moments in the *Star Wars* series.

TIPS & STRATEGY

BEGINNER
STAY COOL

Control your fire when you're using your blaster. It's all too easy to get carried away and overheat it, leaving you unable to defend yourself.

PARTNER UP

When you are teamed up with a Partner, you can respawn on them, instead of at a spawn point. This is really useful for getting close to objectives.

INTERMEDIATE
TEAM PLAYER

Don't focus on your own personal glory. Taking down loads of stormtroopers might make your own stats look good. But if it doesn't help you take the objective and get the win, then what use are "impressive" stats?

DO MORE DAMAGE

Starfighters do more damage when they are traveling slowly, so don't always fly at full speed!

ADVANCED
LEARN YOUR HEROES

Heroes vs. Villains is a great mode to play if you want to learn all the Heroes' and Villains' special abilities, and how best to use them in battle.

LEARN THE MAPS

Look for alternate routes into the main chokepoints. There are often side passages that can help you flank opponents.

CHEATS & SECRETS

BANTHA HUNTER

If you look into the distance while playing on Tatooine, you can spot a herd of Bantha shuffling along through the desert.

CLASSIC CAMEO

Wait long enough on the title screen of *Battlefront* and you'll be treated to a funny little scene involving C-3PO and R2-D2.

TOP 3
Achievements & Trophies

☑ EASIEST ACHIEVEMENT
NEW RECRUIT
Complete any mission
Pick the first training mission that guides you through flying an X-Wing over Tatooine for the easiest route to this Achievement. Lock on with LT and press RB to fire homing missles—this will take out the TIE fighters that you'll come up against, for a quick victory.

ROUND SUMMARY
FOREST MOON OF ENDOR

⬌ TOUGHEST ACHIEVEMENT
DISTINGUISHED
Earn 100 Accomplishments
This one can take a while as you'll need to play a lot of matches. There are 35 different Accomplishments, including defeating enemy players with the same gun ten times, so you'll need to repeat them.

☺ WEIRDEST TROPHY
NOT BAD FOR A LITTLE FURBALL?
Get hit in the head by a rock from an Ewok on Endor
Make sure you're playing as an Imperial and choose Supremacy to play the Forest Moon of Endor map. Hang around the treehouses in the central area of the map until you get lucky and one of the Ewoks gliding above you drops a rock on your head.

FOLLOW THE BATTLE

0   **09:40**   0

DEFEAT THE IMPERIALS

2. ROUND STATUS BAR
Located at the top of the screen, this helpful bit of information is different for every mode. It keeps you up-to-date on which team is in control of the objectives, or is in the lead.

THE MINIMAP
is little map will show you here the opposing team are ing their weapons, helping u hunt them down. Flashing ectors will tell you where to ok, while red dots mean a ero or Villain is nearby.

3. ABILITY STAR CARD
You can also select one Ability Star Card, which provides a special boost or ability (such as a Personal Shield or a Scan Pulse). It could make a big difference in a match.

ACKBAR'S ELITE
COMPLETE ANY SURVIVAL MISSION ON "MASTER" DIFFICULTY WITHOUT DYING

START

BLASTERS
E-11

HANDS
"ROGUE"

"SURVIVOR"
BOWCASTER   ION SHOT   IMPACT GRENADE

"ROGUE"
BARRAGE   COOLING CELL   THERMAL DETONATOR

SELECT A STAR CARD HAND WITH EXTRA GRENADES/ MISSILES
1 Before you start, pick a hand of Star Cards that's good for close-quarters battles (try "Survivor" or "Rogue".) We also suggest using the Hoth map.

FIND A SAFE PLACE TO FIRE FROM
2 When you spawn, turn right and you'll see a small chamber. No enemies will spawn here, so it's a great spot to take out the first wave of enemies from.

GET READY

COLLECTIBLES

4. STAR CARDS

You get to pick three Star Cards for use in each round of *Battlefront*. The ones on the left and right are special items you can use (thermal detonators, jetpacks, etc), but they do need to recharge after each use.

THE EXPERT SAYS...

ELLIOT FÄLTSTRÖM

Known for:
His BattlefrontUpdates YouTube channel

"If you're a new player to *Star Wars Battlefront,* one of the most important things is to play the objectives. Whether it's shutting down an uplink or capturing the cargo, this will gain you more experience and therefore level you up faster! Another good tip is to always stay close to your partner; this will recharge your Star Cards faster and help you defeat more enemies. This effect also applies to objectives, so that's another reason to stay close to the objectives!"

KEEP AT LEAST ONE ENEMY ALIVE

3 Each round asks you to claim a Drop Pod. Don't take out the last Stormtrooper while you're still exposed as defeating them will spawn a new wave of enemies within seconds.

USE TUNNELS AND CANNONS

4 Every three rounds you have to defeat an AT-ST walker. Use grenades, missiles, tunnel entrances, and portable cannons to inflict lots of damage.

LEGO DIMENSIONS

LEGO *Dimensions* brings together some of our favorite franchises—*The Simpsons*, *Ghostbusters*, *Batman*, and a whole lot more—through cool collectible LEGO figures that you place on the Toy Pad to teleport into the game.

TIPS & STRATEGY

BEGINNER ◄
FREEZE FRAME

The Wicked Witch of the West boss can freeze your characters. Pick them up off the Toy Pad and put them down again to unfreeze them.

EASY MONEY

At the beginning of the Wizard of Oz level, turn around and go through the metal gate behind you. You'll find lots of purple studs to give an early boost to your stud count.

INTERMEDIATE ◄◄
TEAMING UP

Finding things tricky? Try getting a friend to jump in with you in co-op and you might find it easier to tackle together.

PAD PUZZLES

Some puzzles require you to move your characters around to certain positions on the Toy Pad. Pay attention to the way the Portal lights up to match what's going on in-game and you should be able to see where to place them.

ADVANCED ◄◄◄
VEHICLE ABILITIES

You don't always have to buy a new character pack to unlock new abilities. All vehicles have three different rebuild options, and they all offer different skills. Earn enough studs and you can open the build, then use the vehicle selection wheel to switch between modes when you need them.

CHEATS & SECRETS

DWARF'S BOUNTY

Select extras and then input the code RY7P8Z to unlock "Dwarf's Bounty," which gives you a x2 stud multiplier.

MEET THE FLINSTONES

In the Melton at Sector 7-G level, a secret TARDIS Station will take you to Fred Flintstone's home!

TOP 4 Achievements & Trophies

☑ EASIEST ACHIEVEMENT

TIME TO BREAK THE RULES!

Rebuild the LEGO Gateway

This will be the first Achievement or Trophy that you unlock. Just move the three characters around the base and hold B or Circle to rebuild the LEGO Gateway.

☺ FUNNIEST TROPHY

BUT DOES IT COME IN PINK?

Give the Batmobile a pink paint job

You need enough studs and bricks to unlock three vehicle tiers and to buy eight circles in the Colors row. Once they're bought, you can use the coloring options to turn your Batmobile pink.

💎 RAREST TROPHY

SPEEDY THING GOES IN . . .

Complete "Aperture Science Enrichment Center" within 25 Minutes

There's a clever cheat you can use here. Play through the level and take as long as you need. When you reach the final boss, choose Exit to Voltron and Save and Quit. Re-enter the level and you'll start at the boss fight.

💎 RAREST ACHIEVEMENT

LOST PROPERTY

Complete 25 Locate Mode Puzzles

You can just solve the same puzzle 25 times to unlock this one. Load "Aperture Science Enrichment Center" and go to the checkpoint in Test Chamber 3. Find and solve the Locate Mode puzzle, then choose Exit To Voltron, Save and Quit. Keep reentering and repeating the puzzle.

GAMER INTERVIEW ▶▶▶

RAY COX

🔊 Known for:
Guiness World Record holder for Gamerscore

AT THE TIME OF THIS WRITING, RAY COX HAS MORE THAN 2,400,000 GAMERSCORE. THAT'S A WORLD RECORD!

How long did it take you to get to the 1 million Gamerscore landmark?
From the start of Achievements—November 2005 when the Xbox 360 launched—it took me eight years and three months to get to exactly 1 million.

How did you feel when you hit 1 million?
The night I knew I was going to hit it, I got really emotional. The fact that I did it live on stream meant that I wanted to get my emotional stuff out of the way first, you know? I didn't want to be like a big baby on screen. Hitting that milestone, though, it was euphoric. This really awesome feeling, knowing that after I put so much time into it I could finally get to that goal. It was one of the greatest feelings and moments for me—I was at peace for a bit, you know? But then you start asking, "What's the next thing I can do?"

Microsoft acknowledged your efforts too, right?
They did, especially around the time I was approaching 1 million. They reached out to me, wanted me to come

Ray is a big fan of the LEGO games, since they are fun to play and easy to complete!

You can download Forza Horizon 2's Fast & Furious expansion to get an easy 1000G.

Cuphead *is the kind of game that Ray loves, with lots of quick Achievements to earn.*

along to their launch event for the Xbox One in Times Square. They gave me the Xbox Live "Gold For Life" subscription, and I think I'm the only person in the world that has that! So they were—and still are—really good to me.

Have you enjoyed every game you've played?

Nope. No way. That said, there are some games that I wouldn't have known about had I not been chasing the Gamerscore—things like the LEGO games. You know, I *love* them now, but before it totally wasn't the kind of thing I'd even want to play. That's the best thing that can come of Achievements or Gamerscore, I think—to discover something new and find something you really love.

What advice would you give to anyone trying to maximize their own Gamerscore?

My advice to people has actually changed over time. Back in the day it used to be super hard to get Gamerscore and all that kind of thing: you'd have to buy a triple-A game for a ton of money or

buy Arcade games and only get 200G each for them. But now you can buy indie games. Indies are *so good* for getting Trophies because you can get 1,000G in about three hours, and they're really cheap as well. Just make sure you always keep an eye on the Xbox Marketplace because they have weekly offers in there. You can pick and complete a lot of indie games in practically no time!

What happened after you hit the 1 million landmark?

Well I'm an "influencer" now—that's the term people have started using for it. But I was doing that kind of thing before it was even really "a thing." People saw my Gamerscore and wanted to catch me and so I was influencing them to play that way. That's kind of what I'm doing now.

Some games will require multiple player but Achievement hunti with friends is great fu

THE WITNESS

This is one of the smartest games you'll ever play. *The Witness* wordlessly teaches you a series of rules through line mazes. When you start to see how they all fit together, you'll feel like a genius.

TIPS & STRATEGY

BEGINNER
GRAB A PEN

Having a pen and paper handy is helpful for solving some of the trickier puzzles. Also try cutting shapes out of graph paper to help you with the game's shape-based puzzles.

COME BACK LATER

The Witness is set on an island, and you can go almost anywhere you like on it, right from the beginning. If you get stuck, just go somewhere else and come back later.

INTERMEDIATE
NEW PERSPECTIVE

Some puzzles are closely tied to what's in the world around them, so pay attention to what you can see in the environment while you're working on a puzzle.

ADVANCED
HAVE A THINK

Try not to get frustrated with complicated puzzles. Stop, sit back, and think about what you know about every symbol in the puzzle and how they affect each other.

DON'T CHEAT

It's tempting to look up the solution to a puzzle when you're stuck, but you should resist. The game's puzzles are teaching you things you need to know, so if you don't understand the solution, you're just going to make the game harder later on!

CHEATS & SECRETS

A NEW BEGINNING

When you've finished the game, restart and take a look at the first gate. Using what you've learned, you can get into a secret area.

TIME FOR REFLECTION

There are loads of perspective-based Easter eggs packed in the game. Try taking a look at reflections in the water, for example.

TOP 4
Achievements & Trophies

☑ EASIEST TROPHY
SYMMETRY

Activate the Symmetry laser

Although the entire island is open from the start, this will likely be the first area you try. The puzzles here are some of the easier ones in the game and the area is close to where you start.

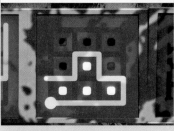

↔ TOUGHEST ACHIEVEMENT
CHALLENGE

Complete a certain challenge

After clearing all other areas and activating all 11 lasers, you go into a secret challenge area. This presents 15 random puzzles that must be solved before the music ends.

🕵 SECRET ACHIEVEMENT
ENDGAME

Reach the end

There are 11 lasers in total but you only need to activate seven of them to see the ending. Which areas you do and which you skip is entirely up to you. Climb the mountain and prepare yourself for a test of everything you've learned up to this point . . .

☺ COOLEST TROPHY
MONASTERY

Activate the Monastery laser

There are a few areas that employ cool new tricks to mix up the line puzzles. This is our favorite—it's a beautiful location, and some solutions require you to think outside of the box to beat them.

KALIMBA

In this clever, color-based platformer, you control a pair of totem pieces. You need to quickly switch between them to get past color-coded obstacles, avoid enemies, and defeat dangerous bosses. It'll test your mind and your reflexes!

TIPS & STRATEGY

BEGINNER
COLOR CODING

Only the green totem piece can move through green areas and only the purple through purple, so look at what's coming up and switch when neccessary.

DOUBLE JUMP

When two totem pieces are stacked on top of each other, you can perform a double jump. Press the jump button a second time when at the top of the first jump's arc for maximum height.

INTERMEDIATE
MAKE A PLATFORM

The pink totem piece has the ability to hover, meaning you can create your own platforms by quickly switching to the other piece. This will make the pink totem stop and hover, so that the other totem piece can then leap onward.

GET IN THE RHYTHM

There's no need to start being overly cautious when you're on ice. It's far easier to slide along quickly and get in the rhythm than it is to try and stop yourself.

ADVANCED
GOLDEN TOTEM

To be awarded a Gold Totem at the end of a level, you need to avoid any failures and get every pickup in the level. Don't worry if you miss one, since levels can easily be replayed from the menu.

CHEATS & SECRETS

SECRET EXIT

Come back down the gravity-switching section at the end of the Jamalry level in the Dark Void DLC for a secret exit.

SECRET ACHIEVEMENT

On the Snakyface level, you can get onto the skeleton arm that's holding up a tree to unlock an achievement.

☑ EASIEST ACHIEVEMENT
UNDYING
Defeat a boss without Dying

The first boss is the easiest for this one. Avoid its attacks and run right. Get to the huge room, wait for the boss to lunge, and then jump onto the glowing parts of its back for an easy takedown.

☺ WEIRDEST ACHIEVEMENT
ILLUMINATI
Reassemble the menu pyramid

Press Down, Down, Up on the pyramid. Only the red and green triangles should move. Now just alternate between Down and Up until the other triangles slot into the pyramid.

SPIRITUAL JOURNEY
COMPANION JOURNEY
UNLOCKABLE POTENTIAL
ACHIEVEMENTS
OPTIONS

☺ FUNNIEST ACHIEVEMENT
THAT'S RIGHT!
Complete a level without dying and always pressing right on the D-pad

The best level for this is "Greenish Vireo." You can even hold right when a small drop forces you to go left. Just remember to hold right *after* the level has loaded so the Achievement doesn't glitch. And don't panic!

♟ CO-OP ACHIEVEMENT
TRUE FRIENDS
Achieve an all-golden co-op totem pole

For this Achievement, you need to grab every collectible on each of the ten co-op levels—without dying. Phew! Both players should learn each level on their own first.

STREET FIGHTER V

Street Fighter V is one of the purest competitive games out there. It isn't just about proving you know your chosen character. It's also about knowing your opponent, too, and predicting and reacting to their moves to come out on top.

TIPS & STRATEGY

REGINNER
STOP JUMPING

Jumping too much is one of the most common mistakes new players make. This is one of the easiest things for a good player to punish, so try staying on the ground rather than constantly jumping.

TEST THE ROSTER

Try out every character to learn their strengths and weaknesses. This will give you a huge advantage when you face off against them.

INTERMEDIATE
USE CROSS-UPS

A cross-up is an attack that hits an opponent from behind, meaning they have to block in the opposite direction than usual to defend it. Cross-ups are great for surprising opponents and keeping them guessing.

KEEP THEM GUESSING

Falling into a predictable pattern makes you easy to beat. Keep your opponent guessing by mixing high and low attacks with throws, cross-ups, and aerial moves.

ADVANCED
LEARN YOUR DISTANCES

Ensuring that you're familiar with how much reach your attacks have helps with poking enemies from a distance and countering effectively when they miss an attack.

LEARN COMBOS

Head into training mode and make sure you've got a couple of combos in your arsenal. You should punish your opponents when they make a mistake, and combos are usually the best way to do that.

CHEATS & SECRETS

ANTI-AIR

Characters have an "anti-air" move for jumping opponents. Ryu has Dragon Punch, Cammy has Cannon Spike, etc.

BE PATIENT

Does your opponent keep throwing projectiles? Jump straight up to avoid them, then walk. Repeat until you're close.

⬌ TOUGHEST TROPHY
BACK FROM HELL

Dare to plunge into Survival Mode on Extreme?

You have to complete 100 fights in Survival Mode on the hardest difficulty with one health bar. It's clear why it's the trickiest challenge in the game—it's *nearly* impossible!

💎 RAREST TROPHY
LET'S FIGHT SOMEONE STRONG!

Finally, Golden League! Now the fun really begins!

You get this Trophy for reaching Golden League in Ranked Matches. You need 4,000 League Points in Online Matches. You lose a lot of LP if you lose a match, so a winning streak is vital.

☑ EASIEST TROPHY
PLAYING FAVORITES

You must set a character as your favorite! Can't decide who to choose? Well, you can't go wrong with Lord Bison!

This is the easiest Trophy in the game and perhaps the easiest you'll unlock in any PS4 game. All you have to do is enter the Battle Setting options from the main menu and then simply set your favorite character.

THE EXPERT SAYS . . .

MATT EDWARDS
Capcom UK Fighting Game Community Manager

Beating 100 AI opponents back-to-back for the "Back To Hell" Trophy is the ultimate endurance test. I know professional *Street Fighter V* players who still haven't bagged this elusive Trophy.

QUICK TIPS & TRICKS

MINECRAFT: STORY MODE

You should talk to everyone you can as much as you can in *Minecraft: Story Mode*. Even if it seems like you have all the useful information you need, keep chatting and you may uncover another secret—or just something that will make you laugh! Keep talking to Reuben at the end of Chapter 3 in Episode 3, while wearing the Enderman suit, and he'll tell you a joke!

GET BETTER AT ONLINE MULTIPLAYER

BE THE BEST WHEN PLAYING WITH FRIENDS ONLINE

Dominating single-player is hard enough. But how do you come out on top when playing multiplayer as well? Going up against human opponents can be terrifying. Human opponents are just like you are—they're unpredictable, they're skilled, and they're dedicated. They're your equal and sometimes, they'll be even better than you.

If you want to be the best gamer you can possibly be, you'll have to embrace the challenge and learn to beat these opponents. Focusing on one particular game can help you excel, so if you want to compete this is a great strategy.

Of course, if you want to play along with your friends and play co-operative multiplayer online, being a good player is still really important. We've got the best strategies and advice to help you be the best, no matter what kind of gamer you are. You'll be winning at online games in no time at all!

THE BIGGEST GAMES

OVERWATCH

This colorful six-vs.-six shooter is one of the biggest online console games around. You choose your character from an eccentric crew that includes gorilla scientists and rollerskating DJs, then do battle against the enemy team.

ROCKET LEAGUE

Rocket League's crazy online multiplayer modes can now be played on Xbox One, PS4, and PC. This means more players than ever before get to try the car-smashing madness of *Rocket League*— including its weird basketball mode.

FIFA 17

FIFA has been one of the most popular online games for many years. Not only do players like the challenge of the main game itself, but also the FIFA Ultimate Team mode, in which you build a dream squad, has also grown in popularity.

FORZA HORIZON 3

The fun *Horizon* spin-off in Microsoft's *Forza* series now offers four player co-op. There are few thrills in gaming to match the four of you skidding around each other in a wide open field, messing around—just because you can.

PLANTS VS. ZOMBIES GARDEN WARFARE 2

What better than a showdown between garden plants and the undead? Not much, if the mayhem here is anything to go by. Success is as much about teamwork as it is individual skill, so rally your friends for some co-op fun!

MINECRAFT REALMS

This awesome multiplayer mode allows you and your friends to play together in a single *Minecraft* world. What's even better is that if your friends are using Windows 10, they can play with you even when you're using the *Pocket Edition*!

IMPROVE YOUR SKILLS

USE IN-GAME COMMUNICATION

You don't always have to use your headset to communicate. Some games have in-game commands for communicating, so use them. If you're playing online, let teammates know what you're planning to do.

CHECK YOUR CONNECTION

Playing online games while your family is streaming TV shows and movies can make your connection slower. If your connection isn't great, take a break and play again later.

PAY CLOSE ATTENTION

If you're playing online, you need to make sure your attention is sharp and focused. Close down any distractions on your laptop or tablet, such as social media.

LISTEN CLOSELY

You gain a lot of information through audio cues—where the enemy is, what weapon they're using, and so on. Using a surround-sound headset or speaker system will give you an advantage when playing onlne.

PRACTICE OFFLINE

If you want to get better at your favorite game, or just try a new tactic, offline modes are the way to do it. Practice in a single-player mode first, then take your new tactics into competitive games when you're confident that you've mastered them.

UPGRADE YOUR CONTROLLER

If you want to get the edge online, you could consider a controller upgrade. Pro controllers offer more responsive buttons, adjustable options, and special paddles to make doing things like reloading much faster.

LEARN FROM LOSSES

When you're playing online, you're bound to run into players who are better than you. Don't get disheartened when you lose to them—just pay attention to their tactics, learn from them, and keep on practicing!

BUDDY UP

Playing online with your friends will dramatically increase your chance of success. You will know each other well and your friends can help you out in close battles, where other online players might leave you on your own.

QUICK TIPS

CHARGE UP
Keep your controller charged and check your battery level before you go online to avoid seeing it switch off mid-game.

CHECK CONTROLS
When you play with a friend, they might change button setups to match their style. Check them before you jump online!

SEE YOUR FRIEND PLAY
In games where co-op isn't possible, watch your friends play in person. You can pick up new tips and tricks.

GET CONNECTED
Move your console closer to your Wi-Fi router, or use an Ethernet cable to get the best connection when playing online.

ONLINE MULTIPLAYER ACHIEVEMENTS & TROPHIES

HALO 5: GUARDIANS

MEDIUM

TOP OF THE FOOD CHAIN
Killed a Legendary Boss in Warzone

To get this Achievement, you need to get the last hit on one of the legendary bosses that spawns during Warzone mode matches. It's easier to get if you jump in with some friends who are happy to stop shooting the boss when it is nearly finished—so you can make sure you deal the final blow.

DIRT RALLY

HARD

EASIER SAID THAN DONE
Finish in the Top Tier of an Online Event

You need to log a time in the top 33 percent of any Daily, Weekly, or Monthly Online Event. You only get one chance at this, so it's best to target Daily events (less competition) and to practice in your own custom offline events before going for the real thing.

FINAL FANTASY XIV: A REALM REBORN

EASY

TO CRUSH 10,000 ENEMIES
Defeat 10,000 enemies

You'll earn this Trophy naturally, as you'll defeat lots of enemies through your time with *Final Fantasy XIV*. If you want to check on your progress, check the Battle tab under Achievements in the menu. And remember, this is for an individual character only. If you switch characters, you'll start again from zero.

Did you know?
The very first *Street Fighter* came out way back in 1987.

STREET FIGHTER 5 **HARD**
SAVORING THE WIN STREAK
Three consecutive victories in Ranked

USE THE STRONGEST CHARACTERS
1 Chun-Li, Nash, and Ryu are considered the strongest characters in *Street Fighter 5*, so fighting as them is a good idea in any match.

FIGHT THE WEAKEST CHARACTERS
2 F.A.N.G. and Zangief are considered the weakest characters, so you should expect to win when these two opponents crop up.

DON'T TAKE NEEDLESS RISKS
3 Try to avoid jumping or throwing fireballs from too close, as these are the two most common mistakes that lead to you taking damage.

ONLINE MULTIPLAYER ACHIEVEMENTS & TROPHIES

STAR WARS BATTLEFRONT

DON'T UNDERESTIMATE THE FORCE

Earn a total of 100 kills while playing as a hero (Multiplayer)

HARD

1. PICK THE RIGHT MODE

Heroes vs. Villains mode is your best bet for this Achievement or Trophy, as you've got a 50% chance of playing as a Hero in every single round.

2. USE YOUR SKILLS

Be aware of the strengths and weaknesses of the Hero you are playing so you can get the best out of them. Han's blaster-based skills mean he can be very dangerous in the open, for example, whereas Luke is better wielding his lightsaber in tighter areas of the map.

3. STICK TOGETHER

When you're playing Heroes Vs. Villains mode, you are safer when you stay with your teammates. Running off on your own and coming up against Darth Vader, Boba Fett, and The Emperor by yourself isn't likely to end well for you!

4. TAKE A RISK

If you're a skilled Battlefront player, try Hero Hunt mode, where it's seven players against one Hero or Villian. If you get the last hit on the Hero or Villain, you get to become one yourself. If you are skilled enough to survive for a long time, you'll rack up tons of kills.

ELITE DANGEROUS

A LONG ROAD AHEAD

Win a CQC Match

MEDIUM

The easiest way to win this challenge is to avoid Deathmatch mode, which places everyone in combat against each other. You can unlock "A Long Road Ahead" in the four-vs.-four Team Deathmatch variant, which gives you a much better chance of winning. All you need to do is win once for this to unlock.

NEVERWINTER
FAITH IN THE FALLEN
Take a leap of faith

 **MEDIUM**

FIND THE TOWER
1 Head to the Tower District and to the coordinates 320, 1168. This will take you to the Fallen Tower Tavern.

HEAD UP
2 Head to the top floor of the tavern, avoiding the enemies dotted around the pathway that leads there.

AND JUMP
3 Jump into the blue light and you'll fall through the tavern and into a secret cave, completing the challenge.

EA SPORTS RORY MCILROY PGA TOUR
PLAYING FOR RANK
Play in a Ranked Online H2H Game

EASY

This is an easy Achievement or Trophy to grab. All you have to do is join a Ranked session from the game's online hub. The best part is you don't even have to play the round, as you'll unlock the Achievement or Trophy right away.

OVERWATCH
NAPTIME
Interrupt an enemy ultimate ability with Ana's sleep dart

MEDIUM

This challenge for newcomer Ana is simple, as long as you focus on the right enemy. You should be playing just away from the action, which keeps you safe from most Ultimates. Look to hit Reaper, Roadhog, or Pharah during their Ultimates, as they are easy targets.

QUICK TIPS & TRICKS

OVERWATCH

You can change your character in the middle of the match in *Overwatch*, when you respawn. However, you should always check your Ultimate meter at the bottom of the screen before you switch. If it's full, or almost full, stick with the same character and use their Ultimate ability on the opposing team. Powers like Mei's Blizzard can often turn a game, but if you switch, your progress in building the meter is lost!

ORI AND THE BLIND FOREST

Filled with gorgeous hand-drawn art, whimsical characters, and a genuinely touching story, *Ori* looks pretty simple at first glance. However, you'll discover some deceptively difficult platforming as you explore its beautiful world.

TIPS & STRATEGY

BEGINNER
REMEMBER TO SAVE

Most modern games save automatically, but *Ori* doesn't. So, don't forget to manually save—especially if you're going into a tricky section.

COLLECT IT ALL

Unlike many games, *Ori*'s collectibles aren't just there for fun! They are used to upgrade Ori's abilites, so make sure you grab any you find.

INTERMEDIATE
WATCH AND LEARN

Every enemy in *Ori* has its own patterns and moves. Pay attention and you can figure out their weaknesses.

TOP TIER SKILLS

The triple jump and shield that you can unlock in the top skill tree are some of the most useful abilities in the game.

ADVANCED
DON'T RUSH

When you are really struggling in the later sections of the game, try not to get frustrated and rush. Look for walls you can use to jump up, and figure out a route before you move.

STOMP 'EM

Stomp is really useful against quick enemies that are tough to hit. It will temporarily stun them, giving you a chance to get some easy hits in.

CHEATS & SECRETS

SECRET AREAS

There are secret areas hidden throughout the game. Keep your eyes open for visual clues.

SUPER MEAT BOY

You can find the character Super Meat Boy hidden in the foreground of the Forlorn Ruins level.

MARIO'S WARP PIPE

A warp pipe from the *Super Mario* series is hidden underwater in the Sunk Glades as a cool referen

☑ EASIEST ACHIEVEMENT
THE JOURNEY BEGINS
Complete the Prologue
It's difficult to play *Ori and the Blind Forest* and not get this Achievement. All you need to do is make it through the game's story-based prologue.

😎 COOLEST ACHIEVEMENT
FLYING FURY
Kill 3 enemies without touching the ground
There are a few places you can do this—anywhere with lots of enemies will do, as long as you're careful. Reflect projectiles with your dodge to stay airborne, or charge your spirit bomb and jump.

🎒 SECRET ACHIEVEMENT
GOOD EYE
Find the lost corridor in the Misty Woods
You'll need to have either restored wind to the forest or unlocked the triple-jump ability if you want to unlock this Achievement. Head all the way to the left in the Misty Woods level to find the secret area and get it.

↔ TOUGHEST ACHIEVEMENT
IMMORTAL
Complete whole game without dying
Ori is a tough game, which makes this challenge almost impossible. If you do die, reloading your previous save won't work unless you quit immediately after dying. Get this to prove you're a real pro.

SHOVEL KNIGHT

It looks, sounds, and plays like a retro game, but this brilliant old-school platformer doesn't feel old-fashioned. That's because it successfully combines the best elements of classic old-school platformers with fresh and funny content.

TIPS & STRATEGY

BEGINNER ◄
SPEND BIG

There's not much point in hoarding your gold since you lose it when you die. Spend it on upgrades instead.

SIGN SLICER

When you're in a village, hit the sign above Molly and potions will rain down. Collect them to refill your magic.

INTERMEDIATE ◄◄
DON'T SKIP ENEMIES

It can be tempting to skip past some of the tougher enemies, but the bigger they are, the more loot they usually drop. That's why it's best to take them on, if you can.

UNTOUCHABLE

Use the Phase Locket on bosses to become temporarily immune to damage. Then get as many hits in as you can!

ADVANCED ◄◄◄
STOP BOUNCING

You can cancel the pogo animation by slashing in the air. This can save your skin when you're about to bounce into danger.

THE GAUNTLET

At the end of the game, try to position yourself in the middle of the battle area after each Gauntlet fight. That way you can quickly grab the food that appears and refill your health.

HEATS & SECRETS

SUPER JUMP

Start a new profile and enter J&2JMP! as your name to play the game with super jump mode activated.

SECRET HUNTING

Look for any walls with icons on and attack them—you might find secrets hidden behind them!

😎 COOLEST ACHIEVEMENT
UNTOUCHED

Emerge unscathed from a battle with any Knight of the Order of No Quarter

Nothing makes you feel like more of a pro than beating a boss in *Shovel Knight* without taking a single hit. The first boss is the easiest for this.

😄 FUNNIEST ACHIEVEMENT
TROUPPLE ACOLYTE

Discover the secrets of the Troupple King

You'll need to visit the Troupple King for this Achievement. Bring a Troupple Chalice, let him fill it up, and then all you need to do is . . . watch him dance. He's got some moves!

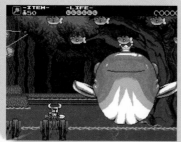

😊 WEIRDEST TROPHY
PENNY PINCHER

Finish the game without spending any money

Going through *Shovel Knight* without spending money is an odd choice, as it means you won't get a lot of upgrades or additional items. You will get this trophy though. Try it on New Game+, as your previous upgrades carry over.

↔ HARDEST TROPHY
IMPOSSIBLE!

Finish the game without dying

This Trophy *is* possible! Beat the game at least once before you attempt a flawless run, and use the Return to Map option if you're about to die.

TEENAGE MUTANT NINJA TURTLES: MUTANTS IN MANHATTAN

The Turtles have their green hands full in *Mutants in Manhattan*, disarming bombs, saving pizza trucks, and more. Whether playing with friends or going solo, you need to combine the unique powers of each Turtle to succeed.

TIPS & STRATEGY

BEGINNER
THANKS, COMPUTER

If you are playing by yourself, let your AI teammates help you out with tougher enemies—especially when you've taken a few hits.

SLOW IT DOWN

Leonardo's ability to slow down time is really useful when attacking. Use it right before you jump into a fight.

INTERMEDIATE
COLLECT ORBS

Most missions aren't timed, so don't rush. Try exploring on your way to an objective to find green orbs that you can use to upgrade your abilities back at the Turtles' lair.

THAT'S TEAMWORK

If you're playing multiplayer, try coordinating your special attacks during boss fights to do massive damage.

ADVANCED
BLOW IT UP

Get a group of enemies near an explosive barrel and then throw a shuriken at it to set it off and do huge damage to the group that is around it.

LEARN TO PARRY

Instead of dodging attacks, you can parry them to leave your opponent wide open for counterattack. It requires expert timing, though, so you're going to have to learn each enemies' attack.

CHEATS & SECRETS

SECRET BOSSES

Return to previously finished levels and there is a chance for a secret boss to appear during boss battles.

DID YOU HEAR THAT?

There are a few lines from the classic TMNT arcade game and original TV series in *Mutants in Manhattan*.

💎 RAREST ACHIEVEMENT
STEALTH MASTER
Complete a stage without being spotted once
Stealth can be tough in this game, which is more action-focused. Use Leonardo (who can slow down time) or Raphael (who can turn invisible) and go to Bebop's residential stage, since it's the easiest one to sneak through.

😄 FUNNIEST TROPHY
PIZZA POSER
Eat a pizza in the snapshots when a boss is defeated
The key here is preparation. You need to bring a boss down to critical health first, then get a pizza ready in your D-pad inventory. Finish the boss off and select the pizza. Your victory snapshot will be of your Turtle eating pizza.

👥 CO-OP TROPHY
NICE TO MEET YOU!
Play online at least once
All you have to do for this Achievement is jump into the online mode and group up with other players. It's a lot of fun to play *Mutants in Manhattan* with friends, so get them involved.

😵 WEIRDEST ACHIEVEMENT
SOOOOAAAAP
Turn all Turtles into zombies simultaneously by touching contaminated water
In the "Armaggon" stage, there's a giant pool of purple, murky water before you encounter the boss. Whether playing with friends or alone, you need to make all four of the Turtles touch this water at the same time.

FUNNIEST
ACHIEVEMENTS & TROPHIES
HOW MANY HAVE YOU UNLOCKED?

Hunting Achievements and Trophies often takes great skill, and a lot of patience. For many gamers, unlocking them is a very serious hobby. However, not every Achievement or Trophy involves beating tough bosses and topping high scores. Sometimes you can be rewarded for playing for laughs.

Crazy stunts and ridiculous actions may actually earn you an unlockable that you never knew existed, and sometimes even dying in the game can reap rewards if you manage to do it with humor. Here are some of the craziest, weirdest, and most hilarious Achievements and Trophies you could ever hope to find!

RAYMAN LEGENDS
AXE SKATER
With Barbara or Elysia, slide on your axe for 100 feet
Xbox One PS4

If you want to smile while playing *Rayman Legends*, then slide! Run at full speed and tap down, then you'll slide until you come to a stop. You can do the same with Barbara or Elysia, who throw their axes onto the ground and slide feet-first on them. The big hill at the start of the game is perfect for a long slide to get this Achievement or Trophy.

THE DEER GOD
TRAIN RIDER
Riding the unexpected train
Xbox One

The Deer God is a game with a powerful message about people versus nature; about a hunter being brought back to life as a deer. You have to interact with different animals to work through the natural environments, and then suddenly, out of nowhere, you have to deal with a train, too! It's so weird seeing this after the calm, peaceful forest that you'll soon find yourself laughing.

LUMO
I DON'T KEN
Perform a Fireball in the Dojo
Xbox One PS4

This is one of the funniest secret Achievements ever—if you get the *Street Fighter* reference! In the virtual environment where you select your controls, do a quarter-circle from down to right on the analog stick, then press A on Xbox One (or X if playing on PS4). It's the same motion Ken uses to do a "Fireball" in the *Street Fighter* series.

OCTODAD
SECRET SHOPPER
Get the Sports Johnson cereal before the lady puts it in her cart

STAY LEFT
1 When you enter the store, stick to the left aisle. Don't worry about being stealthy; just make sure you stay to the left.

TRY NOT TO LAUGH
2 When you see Octodad's limbs flailing around, it'll be hard to concentrate on the game because you'll be laughing so much. Try to stay calm!

CLIMB OVER
3 Climb up and over the shelves when you're about halfway down the aisle, and this will bring you in line with the cereal.

GRAB IT
4 Now just grab the cereal! Don't worry about being precise—just leaning over the shelf in the right area gives you plenty of time to do this.

FUNNIEST ACHIEVEMENTS & TROPHIES

LEGO THE LORD OF THE RINGS
ONE DOES NOT SIMPLY . . .
Walk into Mordor
Xbox One PS4

This line from the *The Lord of the Rings: The Fellowship of the Ring*, has become famous since the first movie in the trilogy appeared. And in LEGO *The Lord of the Rings*, you get the chance to prove Boromir wrong! It's ridiculously simple, too—just travel to the Black Gate with any character, and walk through the gate. It really is that easy, which makes you wonder what all the fuss was about . . .

One doesn't normally think of algae as a dessert item but...um...what the hell.

BACK TO THE FUTURE: THE GAME
LET THEM EAT, UM, CAKE
Treats for all
Xbox One PS4

What's your favorite kind of cake? Strawberry cheesecake? Key lime pie? It's probably not algae cake, but this weird and horrible concoction is what Marty McFly has to give out to everyone at the science expo for this Achievement or trophy to unlock. Surprisingly, some of them even seem to like the slimy, green cakes!

GRIM FANDANGO
"RUN YOU PIGEONS! IT'S ROBERT FROST!"
Try to intimidate the pigeons
PS4

It's not exactly the fiercest battle we've seen in any video game to date—*Grim Fandango's* Manny Calavera versus some pigeons! Yes, your job is to intimidate these skeletal birds, which can only be done with a nearby "Robert Frost" balloon (hence the trophy name) and super-sized dose of courage. It's such a random thing to do that when Manny shouts at the pigeons you're sure to laugh.

LEGO DIMENSIONS

BUT DOES IT COME IN PINK?

Give the Batmobile a pink paint job
Xbox One PS4

Head to the build wheel with 10 gold bricks and 210,000 studs. You need to buy the first eight upgrades in the bottom row for this one. It's pretty funny seeing the normally-serious hero zoom around in a pink car.

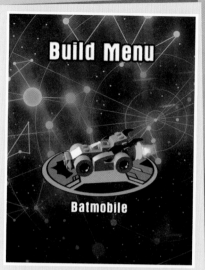

LEGO STAR WARS: THE FORCE AWAKENS

STORMTROOPER SYNDROME

Miss your target 10 times in a blaster battle
Xbox One PS4

This Achievement or Trophy won't have you laughing at the time—in fact you'll probably be a little annoyed at missing your shots! But the reference to the awful shooting skills of the stormtroopers in the original *Star Wars* movies is this game's way of poking a little bit of fun at you. Hey, at least you get something for your continuous failure, right?

I AM BREAD

JOY-RYE-DER

Start the car
PS4

"Joy-rye-der" will be the strangest Trophy you ever unlock. You earn it by starting a car—which is easier than it sounds when you're a piece of bread. You have to flip yourself through a garden, up onto the slide, slide through the driver's window, and land on the keys to get this one.

FUNNIEST ACHIEVEMENTS & TROPHIES

GOAT SIMULATOR
GOATS 'N' STUFF
Hold your own concert
Xbox One PS4

In the "Goat City Bay" map, a hotel dominates the center. If you can make it to the top, you can turn your goat into a dance party DJ by jumping behind the decks. The people on the dance floor will do some hilarious dances!

1. GOAT CITY BAY
To unlock "Goats 'n' Stuff" you must hold your own concert. This means taking over the DJ gig that's taking place on top of the hotel in the middle of Goat City Bay. Load that map and go straight there.

2. JET PACK JOYRIDE
There are two ways to get to the roof of the hotel. Use the Jet Pack goat mutator, which is a little hard to control, or use the mattresses dotted around the outside of the hotel to bounce to the roof.

PORTAL 2
YOU MADE YOUR POINT
Refuse to solve the first test in Chapter 8
Xbox One PS4

This puzzle game is already very funny thanks to the commentary from Wheatley, your dim robot companion. To unlock this particular Trophy or Achievement, make your way to the very first test chamber in Chapter 8 of the game. It's an incredibly easy puzzle—all you have to do is push the button to continue—but to get the Trophy or Achievement, don't do anything. Simply stand still for around 45 seconds and listen as Wheatley gets hilariously agitated by your inactivity!

Wheatley: Designed this test myself. It's a little bit difficult.

KINECT SPORTS RIVALS
CURIOUS
Scan yourself as the opposite gender to your original Champion
Xbox One

Kinect Sports Rivals begins by asking you to scan yourself in with Kinect, so you play as yourself in the actual game. However, for this Achievement, you then have to scan yourself in as the opposite gender. It's pretty funny seeing the game try and figure out how to recreate you!

FUNNIEST ACHIEVEMENTS & TROPHIES

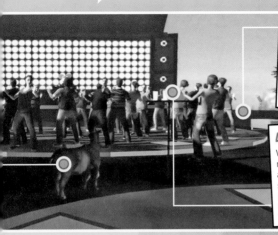

3. BOUNCING BACK

If you do make it to the roof of the hotel without using the elevator that appears near the top floor, you can actually unlock another Achievement or Trophy called "A Story About My Elevator."

4. TIME TO PARTY

When you finally make it to the roof, push through the crowd and get behind the DJ decks to start the party. The crowd will do some crazy dances and you will be rewarded with the "Goats 'n' Stuff" Achievement.

LEGO MARVEL SUPER HEROES
STAN'S SOAPBOX
Turn into Stan Hulk
Xbox One PS4

What's great about this Achievement or Trophy is that it's really a reward for all the hard work you put into the game. Rescue Stan Lee from the "Stan In Peril" moments throughout the game to unlock the Marvel legend. Hilariously, he can turn from a gray-haired man into a giant green monster by holding B or Circle!

STICK IT TO THE MAN
CAREFUL WHAT YOU WISH FOR
Read the mind of a lonely cat
Xbox One PS4

Most cats love attention, so when one is dropped on the floor in *Stick It to the Man*, you can understand its annoyance. Thankfully, in this game you can use your mind-reading powers to hear the cat's thoughts. So, you get to hear his hilarious response—and earn an Achievement or Trophy while you do it.

FIND CHEESE MAN
1 First you have to talk to the guy who thinks he's a piece of cheese, grabbing the dead-mouse sticker right from his thoughts.

FIND THE WOMAN
2 Next you need to bring the dead-mouse sticker to the woman with the cat. The shock will cause her to drop the cat, so you can read its thoughts.

READ HIS THOUGHTS
3 Read the lonely cat's thoughts and see what he has to say. You'll soon realize that this cat is a rather funny creature!

GAMER INTERVIEW

HAKOOM

📢 Known for:
Having the most PlayStation Trophies in the world

Gun.Smoke is Hakoom's proudest gaming success

Most players gave up at the combo trials in *Street Fighter 4*

What made you decide to start hunting down Trophies and Platinums seriously?

As soon as I read about the Trophy patch (which brought Trophies to PlayStation for the first time in July, 2008), I was excited and couldn't wait to play. I wanted to compete and be in the top ten. As soon as I got into the top ten I knew I could end up in first place, because I was going at a very strong pace. It reminds me of the days when I used to play MMOs, back in 2001 to 2006. I always aimed to be at the top.

What do you think separates you as a gamer when compared with other PlayStation owners?

Mostly spirit and determination. I have no limits when it comes to playing and earning Trophies. I grind

Hakoom on *Uncharted 4*: "I cannot explain how much I enjoyed playing this game."

any game until I am able to beat and Platinum it.

How much time do you spend hunting Trophies a week, would you say?

I play a lot. Even when I am asleep I sometimes leave some games running with a turbo controller automatically pressing a button to score or repeat a task for Trophies. I am also married, have a kid, and I enjoy my time with my friends. So there is time for everything.

What Platinum are you proudest of?

I am most proud of my Platinum for *Street Fighter 4* but one game I want to mention, which doesn't have a Platinum, is *Gun.Smoke*. I am more proud of this than any other Trophy

I have earned. The game only has two Trophies and is part of Capcom Arcade Cabinet. It took me two and a half days to finish a 30-minute-long game. It's difficult to explain why, but try it and you will see for yourself.

Are there any types of Trophies you hate trying to unlock?

Yes—many, many Trophies are annoying. I can't stand "collectibles" Trophies. I don't see any use collecting things for a Trophy. Another is grind-fest Trophies. There is no use for that either, it's basically just a waste of time.

Motorstorm was one of the first PS3 games to support Trophies

TRACKMANIA TURBO

This is racing, but not as you know it. *Trackmania Turbo* is one of the hardest racing games out there, asking you to set the best times you can across hundreds of crazy high-octane tracks filled with loops, obstacles, and tight corners.

TIPS & STRATEGY

BEGINNER
FAILING IS FINE

This game is meant to be hard, so treat your first few runs on a stage as a way of getting to know the track, rather than worrying about your lap time.

JUST MOVE ON

If you're really struggling with a track, just move on to another one and come back later. You'll probably find it a lot easier coming back fresh.

INTERMEDIATE
KEEP IT FAIR

If you're playing against a friend, use the random track generator to create a track that neither of you has an unfair advantage on.

TRY A NEW CAR

Each of *Trackmania*'s vehicles handles differently, so it's worth trying different ones out on different tracks and seeing if they can help you improve your time.

ADVANCED
GO FOR GOLD

In single-player mode you can choose to turn on a ghost car that shows you what you need to do to get a gold. Follow it to learn the route.

MASTER THE DRIFT

If you can master the art of drifting your vehicles around corners, it can shave valuable seconds off of your time and help beat your friends' times.

CHEATS & SECRETS

ARCADE SMASH!

Select Multiplayer, then Secret, and press Square, Circle, then any button on PS4 to unlock Arcade Smash! mode.

HOTSEAT SMASH!

Select Multiplayer, scroll down to Secret, press Y, B, then any button to unlock Hotseat Smash! on Xbox One.

😎 COOLEST ACHIEVEMENT
I'M FEELING LUCKY
Create a track with the random generator

Let the random generator in the course creation tool build and save a track for you, and the Achievement is yours.

💎 RAREST TROPHY
GHOST BUSTER
Get at least 50 Trackmaster medals

Trackmaster times are hidden times that go beyond the gold standard on each track. They're secrets, but you'll find most Trackmaster times are two seconds faster than the standard gold time.

👥 CO-OP ACHIEVEMENT
TWO DRIVERS, ONE CAR
Complete a track in double driver campaign

Stay in sync as you both steer the same car! You'll both have to turn the same way to get around tight corners!

↔ HARDEST TROPHY
END OF THE ROAD?
Get a gold medal on every track of the solo campaign

In the earlier levels, gold times are a breeze, but when you hit the black courses, the difficulty really ramps up. The only way to get this is practice, and lots of it.

JUST DANCE 2016

Few games are better at capturing the party atmosphere than *Just Dance*. Packed with some of the best tunes, both new and old, and with a motion control scheme that anyone can use, there's really no excuse not to get dancing!

TIPS & STRATEGY

BEGINNER
USE THE APP

Did you know you can play *Just Dance* using your smartphone's motion control capabilities? Simply download the *Just Dance* app to try it.

TAKE A BREAK

If you're getting tired, you are going to struggle to keep up with the moves, especially with the harder songs. Take frequent breaks.

INTERMEDIATE
TEST RUN

On the first run through a song, focus on getting an idea of the structure of the song and which moves are in it. Don't go for a high score.

LEVEL UP

It's tempting to stick to the songs you play well, but you'll never improve if you don't test yourself with songs that you struggle with sometimes.

ADVANCED
BREAK IT DOWN

Break a song down into its individual dance moves and practice each one to make sure you've got them down before putting it all together.

LEARN THE SONG

When you're going for perfect ratings and high scores, it helps a lot if you know the song by memory, rather than having to react quickly to on-screen instructions.

CHEATS & SECRETS

RAVING RABBIDS

The Raving Rabbids from the *Rayman* series first made a cameo in *Just Dance 2*.

THE MORE THE MERRIER

Unlock the extreme version of *Barbra Streisand* in *Just Dance 3* by using the Konami code on the start screen.

☑ EASIEST ACHIEVEMENT
WELCOME TO JUST DANCE 2016!
Complete your first song

Simply finish your first song in *Just Dance* and you'll earn your first Achievement along with it. It's as easy as that!

⬌ TOUGHEST TROPHY
COMPLETE YOUR JOURNEY
Finish first on all the Dance Quests with a Hard difficulty

Just Dance's Dance Quests aren't for noobs. You'll need to bring your dancing A-game to conquer them all, especially on Hard difficulty. Move and shake your way to the top and you'll earn this tricky Trophy.

◉ COOLEST TROPHY
PERFECT FINISH!
Get a Perfect on the last move of a song (No Mash-Ups)

It doesn't matter if your routine goes wrong in the middle, if you nail your finishing move you'll still look like a dancing superstar. Get a Perfect on the final move to earn this Trophy.

☺ FUNNIEST ACHIEVEMENT
FOREVER ALONE
Dance to a 2-Dancer song on your own

Sometimes you're in the mood for a duet, but there's nobody to dance with you. Not to worry—you'll get this Achievement for finishing a two-dancer song by yourself.

FIFA 16

For fans of soccer, it's the unmatched realism in every detail that makes the *FIFA* series stand out. From the faithfully recreated stadiums, to the brilliant match-day presentation, playing as your favorite team is a special soccer experience.

TIPS & STRATEGY

BEGINNER ◄
GET CHEMISTRY

Try to link up players of the same nationality or that play for the same club in real life. This will boost your team's chemistry in Ultimate Team.

KEEP YOUR SHAPE

You shouldn't always rush out to close attackers down. It you leave big gaps in your defense, it will be easy for your opponents to exploit.

INTERMEDIATE ◄◄
MIX IT UP

Vary your passing in *FIFA* to pull defenders out of position and get in behind the defensive line. Mix short passing with long balls and through balls.

TIME FOR CHANGE

If you're struggling in a match, try making a tweak to your formation or tactics. It can make a big difference.

ADVANCED ◄◄◄
FEINT

Feints are one of the most effective ways of fooling your opponent. Use feint crosses on the wing and feint shots on the edge of the box to make space for your player.

LEARN THE SKILLS

Head into Practice mode and practice some tricks and skills that you can use to improve your dribbling. This will help you go past opposition players much more easily in a game.

CHEATS & SECRETS

ALIEN ABDUCTION

FIFA 2000 had an alien mode where aliens would try to abduct players from the field by beaming them up!

LOOK CAREFULLY . . .

In *FIFA 14*, every cameraman had an image of a Man Utd vs. Liverpool game on their camera's screen.

TOP 4
Achievements & Trophies

⬌ TOUGHEST ACHIEVEMENT
THE INVINCIBLES

Win all 4 matches in an Online FUT Draft session in FIFA Ultimate Team

Winning four FUT games is a tough task, but doable. It does take a bit of luck, though . . .

☑ EASIEST ACHIEVEMENT
WE'RE IN THE GAME

Play a women's match

EA has celebrated the first ever inclusion of professional female soccer players in a *FIFA* title by adding this Achievement. Simply finish a women's match to unlock it.

👥 MULTIPLAYER TROPHY
FRIENDSHIP TEST

Finish an entire Online Friendlies Season

The Online Friendlies mode lets you play one-on-one against a friend over a series of matches. Whoever has the most points wins, you just need to play right up to the end of the season.

🎮 WEIRDEST TROPHY
JUST A LITTLE OFF THE SIDES

Change your haircut

When creating your Pro player, you'll see a range of haircuts. Earn a Trophy by going back and changing your hairstyle in any way.

MADDEN NFL 16

EA's popular football franchise just seems to get better every year, but you don't have to be a veteran player to rack up the touchdowns. Here's how to play like a pro in the latest version of *Madden*...

TIPS & STRATEGY

BEGINNER
MIX IT UP

Some plays might seem extremely effective, but using them too much will cause opponents to get wise. Keep the other guys guessing!

PASSING PRACTICE

If your passing game isn't up to speed, put in some practice. Running plays can work well, but you need to be able to mix in passing play.

INTERMEDIATE
THE BEST QB

Looking for the best quarterback for your Ultimate Team? You won't find better than Aaron Rodgers—he's the highest rated QB in the game!

KEEP IT LOW

Low passes are harder to intercept, so use L2/LT to throw a tricky pass to a receiver in space if you're worried about an interception.

ADVANCED
CONTAIN RUNNERS

If you're up against a quarterback who favors running plays, use "Contain Assignment" (LT+RB/L2+R1) to put two defenders on him.

MASTER THE PLAYBOOK

Expert players use the full extent of their playbooks, so don't be afraid to bust out some crazy unexpected plays!

CHEATS & SECRETS

EASY CASH

Low on funds? Hit the Solo Challenges for a quick and easy way to top up your balance to grab new packs.

KEEPING THE BALL

Running moves can now be enhanced with R2/RT or L2/LT, perfect for breaking away from a strong defense.

⊙ COOLEST ACHIEVEMENT

SATISFYING COMEBACK

Win even if you're trailing by 17+ points at halftime

To make a stunning comeback, keep hold of the ball with short passing and you'll come out on top!

☑ EASIEST ACHIEVEMENT

LAB RAT

Change one or more penalty sliders in the settings menu

For this to pop, head to the settings and find the Penalty option. Adjust the sliders and save your option. You can always change it back once the Achievement is unlocked.

🎲 SECRET TROPHY

WHY NOT ME IN THE SUPER BOWL?

Make it to a MUT Seasons Super Bowl

Be careful with your coins and be patient on your way to building a team good enough to make it all the way to the Super Bowl game.

◆ RAREST TROPHY

THREW DOWN THE GAUNTLET AGAIN

Defeat the Level 25 Boss of the Skills Trainer Gauntlet

To beat the final boss, redo all the previous skill games and beat each score.

NBA 2K16

As the most realistic basketball game ever made, *NBA 2K16* can be overwhelming in the amount of controls and options it offers players. Put in the time, though, and you'll eventually emerge as a slam-dunking all-star!

TIPS & STRATEGY

BEGINNER ◄
SHOOTING DRILL

Work on your shot timing in training before taking to the court and embarrassing yourself—you'll want to make the most of each opportunity.

CONTROL FREAK

There's a lot to take in, but go through the complete control list and try to commit as much of it as possible to memory. You'll be glad you did it.

INTERMEDIATE ◄◄
A NEW ANGLE

Try switching from the broadcast camera to one that looks down the court—passes are easier to aim and you can spot breaks and runs better.

POSTING UP

Check your players' stats—those with high Post Control can hit easy baskets by turning their backs on defenders with L2/LT and shrugging them off.

ADVANCED ◄◄◄
MANUAL DRIBBLING

Want to keep possession and look good doing it? Dribble skills—activated with various right stick directions and combos—help do just that.

FINDING RUNES

Examine every MyTEAM card to try and find rare Runes near the card's Overall stat. Find five of these and you'll get access to the Black Market.

CHEATS & SECRETS

Keep an eye on 2K's various social media channels for codes that you can use to unlock extra content.

Enter the following Locker Code in the menu to unlock Shaquille O'Neal: GSUM3 ESARX GXD3T S3QJQ FIETU

TOP 4
Achievements & Trophies

☑ EASIEST TROPHY
JUST SAY NO
Purchase a Card Pack in MyTEAM mode

By buying one of the packs of cards in MyTEAM mode, you can add new players, skills, and fitness cards. The more you play, the more points you'll get to spend on these.

⊖ COOLEST ACHIEVEMENT
BUZZER BEATER
Make a winning shot with no time left on the clock

Although it takes a lot of luck to get this shot timed correctly, it's definitely one of the coolest Achievements we've seen in a while. Make sure you're either tied, or losing by a single point, then take your shot with around two seconds left on the clock.

⬌ HARDEST ACHIEVEMENT
PERFECTION
Win all 10 games of "Greatest of All-Time" in Play Now Online

In the "G.O.A.T" games, you'll be up against the best players with advanced skill sets. It's a tough competition, so you'll need to have a solid defensive game to stand a chance of winning.

🎴 SECRET TROPHY
FORTUNE HUNTER
Acquire all runes in MyTEAM

There are 30 runes in the MyTEAM mode, attached to current and historic players. You need a degree of luck to draft these players, though.

THE FASTEST GAMES TO 100% COMPLETE

GET YOUR QUICK FIX AND FINISH IN THE FASTEST TIME

20

GRIM FANDANGO

The HD remaster of a classic point-and-click puzzle game is unique and hilarious. Best of all, it gives up all its Trophies as a reward for completing fun tasks, such as scaring the living and having someone recite one of your poems.

THE LEGO MOVIE VIDEOGAME

It usually takes a while to acquire every last unlockable Achievement or Trophy from a LEGO game. The exception is *The* LEGO *Movie Videogame*, clocking in at a modest 10 hours. This might sound like a long time, but the game is a lot of fun. You don't have to finish in one play, either!

19

VALIANT HEARTS: THE GREAT WAR

This moving puzzle game about the brave men and women in World War I takes only a few hours to finish. You'll learn a lot about the war while you play, and the game itself is excellent, with creative bosses and a touching story.

18

17

BACK TO THE FUTURE: THE GAME

The game is split over five episodes that each take a few hours to complete. The puzzles are all pretty simple, especially if you've seen the movies.

COSTUME QUEST 2

16

If you play with the Candy Corn costume equipped, you can unlock everything in this cutesy action game with one playthrough. Some of the challenges are fun too, such as honking the clown horn 1,000 times. It's probably not much fun for anyone having to listen to you play it, though!

STICK IT TO THE MAN

15

This unusual combination of puzzle game, stealth sneaking, and platforming is one of the weirdest games you'll ever play. It's possibly one of the shortest, too—you can complete it in roughly four hours. Use chapter select to go back and collect any Achievements or Trophies you might have missed.

STRIDER

14

This modern reboot of an old retro classic has lots of collectibles to find, which can be quite hard. However, those with quick reactions and nimble fingers can smash through *Strider* in three hours. In fact, you have to complete it this quickly to unlock one of the Achievements or Trophies.

PNEUMA: BREATH OF LIFE

It will take roughly three hours to work through this first-person puzzle game, with an extra hour to return and complete any puzzles you might have missed. That means that you can grab all of the Achievements and Trophies from *Pneuma* in around four hours—probably less if you're really smart!

13

12
GIANA SISTERS: DREAM RUNNERS

Don't get this confused with *Giana Sisters: Twisted Dreams*, which is difficult and time-consuming! In *Dream Runners*, you have to beat your opponents in a race to force them off the screen. Doing this on every map will unlock every Achievement and Trophy, and should only take a few hours.

11
BROTHERS— A TALE OF TWO SONS

You might need to use a guide to make sure you don't miss any of the Achievements or Trophies in this puzzle-platformer, but they aren't tough to unlock. It's a cinematic adventure, and it's lots of fun—which is a nice bonus!

KNIGHT SQUAD

There are only 15 Achievements and Trophies in this game, meaning you should be able to complete this game very quickly. Connect a second controller and play in custom multiplayer games without a real opponent to make things easier, and unlock everything even faster.

9
6180 THE MOON

In this cute platformer, you play as the Moon trying to visit the Sun to ask him why he isn't rising. It gives up all its Achievements in three hours, and they're all easy to unlock. You can complete it even faster than that if you're skilled— the record time is 10 minutes!

10

#IDARB

8

There are lots of easy Achievements in this crazy mashup of pixels, platforming, and putting the ball in the goal. You should unlock them all within a few hours. They include some of the most creative Achievements in gaming, such as making your own victory song!

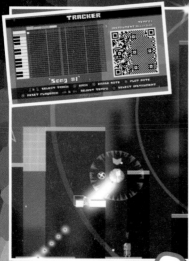

7

CONTRAST

Not only is this platformer gorgeous to look at, but it's easy, too. You can complete *Contrast* in four hours—maybe fewer if you're a pro gamer. Use "Chapter Select" to mop up any Trophies or Achievements you've missed.

THE SWAPPER

6

There's a secret terminal hidden in every level, and *The Swapper* gives you an Achievement or Trophy each time you find one. In fact, these are the only Achievements offered. You have to be smart and resourceful to uncover the hidden terminals, but finding them all won't take longer than four hours.

5

ANOTHER WORLD— 20TH ANNIVERSARY EDITION

This modern re-release of an old retro classic tests a variety of your gaming skills. However, it's short, and you can reach the end credits in just a few hours. Look out for the secret UFO at the start to get an Achievement or Trophy. Miss it and you'll have to start again!

THOMAS WAS ALONE

4

This unique platforming adventure takes only a few hours to play through, and it's a lot of fun. You can head back into any level from the main menu to find any Trophies you missed, making this one of the fastest games to fully complete on Xbox One and PS4.

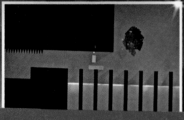

3

FORZA HORIZON 2 PRESENTS FAST & FURIOUS

This extra downloadable content for *Forza Horizon* gives up its 1,000 Gamerscore in little more than two hours. There aren't many Achievements, and they're all really easy (and fun) to unlock!

MONOPOLY PLUS

2

If you're really smart and bend the rules to your advantage, you can grab all the Achievements or Trophies in as few as two games. Try playing with House Rules and restarting the game until you get the first go—that way it will only take a couple of hours to 100%.

BEYOND EYES

1

Beyond Eyes is the perfect game for those wanting super-fast Achievements and Trophies. It's easy to play, quick to complete, and unlike any other game you might have played. You play as Rae, a blind girl trying to find her missing cat, and exploring the world using sound and touch. The pace is calm, and Achievements reflect the gentle nature of the game: feeding cows by hand, escorting chickens across a bridge, sitting on a swing, and so on. Not only is it the quickest game to 100% complete, but it is also a unique gaming experience.

QUICK TIPS & TRICKS

NO MAN'S SKY

The ultimate goal of *No Man's Sky* is to reach the center of the universe, so it may be tempting to simply point your ship in that direction and go. If you do this, though, you'll miss out on undiscovered planets, ship upgrades, and some really cool creatures. Take your time, get some upgrades, and when you're ready, you can head for the final goal!

Olufjornerens

Undiscovered

440,534ks
Arrive in   00:04:59

RRIVE IN: 5:18
ANUFACTURING FACILITY

Rasamama S36

SHIELD

Manufacturing Facilities contain new C

Abandoned

DIRT RALLY

The series had been slowly creeping farther and farther from the traditional rally action that started it all, but the latest game is a stunning return to form. Be warned, though—the tough handling model doesn't pull any punches!

TIPS & STRATEGY

BEGINNER
SLOW START

Dirt Rally is an extremely difficult game and one that will take a fair amount of practice to master. Pick a slow car like the Mini while you're learning.

CHOOSE A VIEW

Some players prefer the thrill of the cockpit view, while others like to race from behind the car. Try out both, and use whichever works best for you.

INTERMEDIATE
LISTEN AND LEARN

Stages are complex, so you can't really expect to learn them. Instead, pay attention to your co-driver, who will tell you what is ahead.

UNDER THE HOOD

When making any major changes to your car, it helps to do them one at a time. This allows you to get a better feel for the impact each one has.

ADVANCED
USING THE E-BRAKE

Smart use of the handbrake can shave seconds off your times, but remember that it's best used to get more turning power at lower speeds.

SLIP AND SLIDE

The Scandinavian Flick is a pro technique where you oversteer while approaching a tight corner, then use your momentum to slide into and exit it as tightly as you can.

HEATS & SECRETS

A QUICK BUCK

The fastest way to earn money is with Hill Climb events on Master difficulty. This can bring in over $100k every few minutes.

RACER REBOOT

If an AI rival is performing particularly well, quit the game. They may put in a worse stage time if you try again.

TOP 4
Achievements & Trophies

⬌ TOUGHEST ACHIEVEMENT
BORN TO RUN
Became Champion at Masters level in Championships.

There's no shortcut to getting this Achievement, unfortunately. You're just going to have to get really good at the game.

☑ EASIEST ACHIEVEMENT
OBVIOUSLY
Bought A Rally Car

Dirt Rally is a tough game to beat, but it does have a softer side. You can't do anything without buying a car, and as soon as you do, you'll unlock an Achievement. From there it gets a little more difficult.

⊕ COOLEST TROPHY
NAILED IT!
Roll your car, land on your wheels and carry on

There's a decent chance you'll get this Trophy by accident when just playing through the game. If not, you need to try to catch the lip of a slope to send your car into a barrel roll. Catching the angle just right might require a few tries and a bit of luck.

☺ WEIRDEST TROPHY
MONDAYS BE LIKE
Crashed your car so badly it ended your rally

If you wreck your vehicle to such an extent you can't finish the race, you'll get a Trophy. It's a fun one to go for!

FORZA MOTORSPORT 6

Microsoft's flagship racer continues to set the bar for the genre. It's a reliable franchise that consistently delivers superb on-track action. Between this and the *Horizon* spin-off series, you may never need another racing game.

TIPS & STRATEGY

BEGINNER
HELP WITH HANDLING

FF (front wheel drive), FR (rear wheel drive) and AWD (four-wheel drive) cars all handle differently. Experiment with all three to see if you prefer the understeer of FF, the drift-friendly oversteer of FR or the additional traction of AWD.

INTERMEDIATE
NO GOING BACK

Rewinds let you fix your mistakes, but should be used sparingly. Disabling them entirely grants a healthy 10 percent boost to race earnings. Sometimes, though, it's worth sacrificing that in longer races, where there's more chance of making an error.

HEAD TO THE HUB

Forza Hub is an Xbox One companion app that tracks your progress across all games in the series and rewards you with *Forza* credits and cars for hitting various milestones. It's a free download, so there's no reason not to download it and enjoy the benefits.

ADVANCED
TURN OFF ASSISTS

As you learn the courses, try to gradually disable Driving Assists one by one. Doing so will grant you an income boost, and it's the best way to fully appreciate the incredible simulation of real racing that developer Turn 10 has created.

CHEATS & SECRETS

WICKED WHEELS

Looking for a great ride on the cheap? Check out the Corvette Z06 or the TVR Sagaris—neither will break the bank and both are superb rides.

ANYONE FOR SHRIMP?

Drive a few hundred meters to the roundabout on the Long Beach track. Turn around to see the Bubba Gump Shrimp restaurant from *Forrest Gump*!

◎ COOLEST ACHIEVEMENT
CAR CULTURE
Complete a Race with every car from Ferrari

Can you imagine anything more fun than speeding around racing tracks in Ferraris? That's all you have to do here—you don't even have to win!

⬌ TOUGHEST ACHIEVEMENT
CHASE CAR
Lead For 100 Miles

Trying to stay out in front for 100 miles can be time-consuming. A single mistake can cost you the lead in some races, but just keep going. Eventually, with enough races, your distance will add up to 100 miles.

☑ EASIEST ACHIEVEMENT
POSTING A SELFIE
Share a Photo

Take a photo of anything and share that photo. That's all you have to do! With this, you can rack up an extra Achievement almost instantly.

👥 CO-OP ACHIEVEMENT
CASHING IN
Earn 50,000 credits from the community using your Design

It may not be co-op as we know it, but submitting a livery design to *Forza*'s hub and earning credits from other players using it feels great. It's like being part of a gaming community!

FARMING SIMULATOR 15

You wouldn't think something as everyday as farming would make for a great game, but this satisfying farming sim proves otherwise. Its relaxing pace makes it great for winding down after some high-octane action.

TIPS & STRATEGY

BEGINNER
EASY MONEY

By placing multiple solar collectors and windmills, turning off plant growth, and accelerating game time, you'll earn money insanely fast. So just place some down, leave your game idle, place a few more, and repeat. Then enjoy your free money!

COUNTER-WEIGHTS

Smaller, lighter tractors don't deal well with pulling heavy equipment. But instead of investing in a new tractor, just add weights to the front of your existing one to correct the balance cheaply. This will save your cash for when you really need it.

INTERMEDIATE
SPEED FARMING

Once you understand the regular needs of your farm and can manage them easily, crank up the game speed to get things moving more quickly. If you struggle to get everything done, just drop back to a lower setting until you catch up.

ADVANCED
STAY INFORMED

Make sure you regularly check your PDA. With information on current prices, the status of your fields, and a whole lot more, it gives you the vital information you need to plan and manage your farm with maximum efficiency.

CHEATS & SECRETS

SAVE EDITING

On PC, you can open your save file, search for "money," and edit the value to get as much as you want. Sneaky!

CASHING IN

Collect all 100 gold coins and visit the well in the bottom left corner of the map to unlock a hidden treasure.

☑ EASIEST ACHIEVEMENT
NOUVEAU-RICHE
Your account has reached more than 1 million.

Farming Simulator isn't meant to be hard, so while reaching more than 1 million sounds like a lot, it's really not. Using our "Easy Money" tip, you'll hit the milestone in no time.

☺ WEIRDEST ACHIEVEMENT
FINANCIAL FOLLY
You managed to reach a negative balance on your very first day

The idea of the game is to make money, so it's weird that there's an Achievement for doing the opposite! Hire workers when you're close to zero to get into debt.

⊜ COOLEST TROPHY
LUMBERJACK
You cut down 50 trees in one game with a chainsaw or a wood harvester

Farming isn't all about crops. You also cut down trees with a chainsaw. Not only is the chainsaw fun to use, it gets you this Trophy, too.

⬌ TOUGHEST TROPHY
MISSION MASTER
You have completed 50 missions

You can pick up missions that ask you to perform specific tasks from boards dotted around the map. Try to have a diverse farm so that you can deliver on whatever you are being asked for in each mission you take on.

HALO 5: GUARDIANS

Microsoft's biggest FPS has been at the forefront of Xbox since the first console launched, and the series continues to get stronger and stronger. *Guardians* is one of the best yet—especially the excellent multiplayer mode.

TIPS & STRATEGY

BEGINNER
CONTROL FREAK

With plenty of different control schemes available, there's bound to be one that's right for you. Make sure you're happy with your choice before you really get into the game— relearning a new setup after some time with the game can be quite the headache.

DRESS TO IMPRESS

Do you want to unlock some new gear? Three classic sets of armor are available for unlocking various Achievements in *The Master Chief Collection*, while the *Nightfall* set can be earned simply by having watched all five episodes of the TV series.

INTERMEDIATE
THE THIRD SKULL

Struggling to find the Skull on mission three? That's probably because it's only available on Legendary difficulty. Shoot down the fighter attacking the cargo ship with your tank's turret, and a Skull will spawn.

ADVANCED
MASTERING MELEE

The two new melee options can be tricky to use. The shoulder bash is a powerful charge that can be used only when you've hit your top sprint speed. The ground pound allows you to jump up and aim your shot—it's more deadly when used from higher up.

HEATS & SECRETS

THIRSTY?

In mission 3, activate the Blu Soda vending machine three times and you'll get a free gun. Repeat for more weapons!

THE SINGING GRUNT

Leap over the wreck at the start of mission seven. Follow the path to find a Grunt sitting on the cliff, singing happily.

😎 COOLEST ACHIEVEMENT
FIRE DRILL

Finished Evacuation within 18:00 without dying on Heroic difficulty

This test of skill really shows off your *Halo* credentials. Your friends will have to respect your skills if you manage to get this one.

☑ EASIEST ACHIEVEMENT
YOUR STYLE

Changed your Spartan's gear in the Spartan Hub

All you need to do to bag this Achievement is head into the Customization menu and then switch your armor, helmet, visor, or color. Exit the menu to be given the Achievement.

😄 FUNNIEST ACHIEVEMENT
ON MY MARK

Simultaneously assassinated two Elites in Blue Team co-op

This Achievement tasks you with working with a pal to eliminate two Elites at the same time. You'll be laughing—and arguing— at how wrong it can go . . .

👥 CO-OP ACHIEVEMENT
ALL FOR ONE

Completed every co-op Mission on Heroic difficulty

The key to this Achievement is to not play the game like you would in single-player. Work together and make sure you are always communicating to manage your enemies successfully.

CHEATS & TIPS FOR BEATING THE GAME!

FOR THOSE WHO NEED A SHORTCUT . . .

Your thumbs have permanent pad indents pressed into them, you have the reactions of a cat, and you've survived intense battles, online and offline. However, even for an experienced gamer like yourself, there are some games that can be nearly impossible to finish without assistance. Even the best players need a helping hand sometimes.

That's where these tips, tricks, and cheats come in. The shortcuts you'll find on the following pages will put you on the fast track toward success for some of the trickier games ever made. So let us help, and you'll take your gaming to a whole new level.

GUACAMELEE! SUPER TURBO CHAMPIONSHIP EDITION

UNLOCKING HARD MODE

Save yourself time with this quick cheat

Ordinarily, you would have to complete *Guacamelee!* to unlock Hard Mode. Fortunately, there's a cheat to save you some time, if you want to test your skills straight away at the tougher difficulty. Press Left, Right, Left, Right, Square, Triangle, Square, Square, SELECT. On Xbox One, press Left, Right, Left, Right, X, Y, X, X, View. This unlocks Hard Mode so you can jump straight into it.

DRAGON BALL: XENOVERSE
EARNING EASY MONEY
How to gather 500,000 zeni

Once you've collected all seven Dragon Balls, summon Shenron and tell him you want money. When a dialog box appears saying you've got 500,000 zeni, don't press OK. Instead, press the Home button and sign out. Then go back to *Dragon Ball: Xenoverse* and sign back in. You'll still have all of your Dragon Balls, plus an Achievement!

CASTLE CRASHERS REMASTERED
CLIMB THE LEADERBOARDS
How to survive in a Back Off Barbarian match

1. FLAT MAP

Back off Barbarian is the toughest mode but here's a clever trick. Start by picking any flat map to play on.

2. MASH THE BUTTONS

With a second player in tow, you just need to mash the face buttons. Mash them quickly, to move as fast as possible.

3. CAN'T TOUCH THIS

This moves you so quickly that the AI can't keep up. You'll survive long enough to post an amazing time.

DIRT RALLY
SURVIVE EVEN THE TOUGHEST CORNERS
How to stay on the track in this challenging game

The trick to doing well in racing games is to take corners as wide as you can, so you can cut into the corner while maintaining speed. However, that's not the case in *Dirt Rally*. Some corners are littered with dirt, debris, and obstacles on the outside, and clipping them will send you flying off the track. Always listen to your co-driver. He'll warn you about any debris and you'll know if it's safe to drift wide or not.

FINAL FANTASY X HD
BLITZBALL MASTER
Unlock all slot reels

You need to earn three slot reels as Blitzball rewards, and there's an easy way to win Blitzball matches. When you're winning, swim behind your goalkeeper or on the right side of the arena and everyone else will start swimming in circles. Just stay there to run down the clock. If someone on the other team gets too close, break through him and then he'll join the rest of his team again. You can also pass between your own team to rack up XP points.

LEGO THE HOBBIT
QUITE A MERRY GATHERING
Collect all characters

There are 98 characters to collect in LEGO *The Hobbit*, but you can save time unlocking the characters below by entering the following in the Enter Code section in the Extras menu:

Alfrid	FAVZTR
Azog	84ZZSI
Bain	W5Z6AC
Bard	UER3JG
Barliman Butterbur	XTVM8C
Barrow Wight	555R9C
Beorn	KEID2V
Bolg	ZIBYHO
Braga	MXUXKO
Elros	H2CAID
Fimbul	THAVRM
Galadriel	00TE7J
Gollum	3CE37P
Grinnah	TPD7YW
Lindir	V4Y5HZ
Master of Laketown	9NOK35
Narzug	4FYKKB
Necromancer	NM3I2O
Percy	74KN31
Peter Jackson	5OJEUC
Rosie Cotton	TB4S6J
Sauron	OARA3D
Thror	SYKSXF
Tom Bombadil	4Y95TJ
Witchking	V8AHMJ
Yazneg	S6VV33

NBA 2K16
BIG COMEBACK
How to snatch victory from the jaws of defeat

Mounting a comeback in *NBA 2K16* can be done with clever play. When there are only a few minutes left, put your best 3-point shooters on the court. Then start playing aggressively for steals. If you steal the ball, this will lead to a fast break, which will be a quick two points. If you don't get the steal, then when you do get the ball back, pass the ball around the 3-point line until a shot opens up.

PROJECT CARS
GET AHEAD OF THE PACK
Use valuable information from your race engineer to beat the pack

While you race, you'll have information fed to you by your race engineer. Always listen to what he says. Your race engineer will tell you about gaps opening up in front or behind you, and always tells you when to push harder. But most importantly, you'll get weather information. Always act on this information, so you can change your tires before the weather changes. You don't want to get caught out when it starts raining!

TERRARIA
BLOOD MOON APPEARS
Summon and survive the secret event

There's a small chance of a secret event called Blood Moon appearing during the night if you have over six hearts of health. How do you survive when it happens? Bury yourself in a small box of stone and wait for 4.30 a.m., when the Blood Moon event ends.

ROCKET LEAGUE
FAST BREAK
How to dominate the unusual "Hoops" mode

1. SHOOTING HOOPS
Rocket League fans will have squeezed everything they can from this mashup of car, rockets, and soccer by now. But the *Hoops* DLC adds a new basketball mode and brings brand new challenges with it.

2. STICK TO THE OUTSIDE
Try to "dribble" the ball around the outside of the court, where there are fewer cars and less action. Use a gentle shot toward the opponent's hoop when you want to score.

3. WHEELS FIRST
Hoops mode will see you spending more time than normal in the air, so it's especially important to make sure you land on your wheels. Landing on your roof wastes a few seconds as you tip your car back over.

4. DRIVE THROUGH THE NET
Remember that you can drive through your own hoop to stop the opponent from scoring, If you're sharp, you can even turn this rebound into a quick attack down the court.

WWE 2K16
WE HAVE A NEW CHAMPION!
How to win the WWE Championship

This is much easier than it seems, as long as you stay out of any feuds until the "Money In The Bank" event in June. Win that match and then perform a run-in and you'll be given the option to cash in your briefcase. Accept this option. Whoever the champ is will have no health at all, making this fight the easiest way to become the WWE Champion.

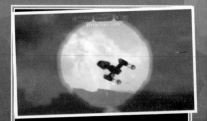

STAR WARS BATTLEFRONT
DESTROY Y-WINGS
How to take out Y-Wings in Walker Assault

In Walker Assault mode on Outpost Beta, jump up the left side of the map and enter the door *before* you reach the hangar door. Go down the hall, turn right and out the hangar door, and jump in the DF-9 turret. The Y-Wings turn up five to six minutes into the round. Destroy them with one shot. They arrive in three waves and will take the same path every time.

TRIALS FUSION
EARN A MONSTER SCORE
Score 20,000 points from one jump on a FMX track

1 CATCHING AIR
On the "Airtime" map, race through as normal without doing any tricks, but stop before the last propeller (deliberately crash if you need to slow down.) Slowly inch over the last propeller, so you keep bouncing up.

2 20,000 POINTS INTO THE SKY
Now hold any trick in this position and keep flipping, until your score hits the necessary 20,000 points. This counts as a single jump.

3 AND FINISH
Finally, bail off your bike on the ramp to the left and wait for the time to expire, so you collect the 20,000 points for one jump.

GODZILLA
FINISHED IN 6
Clear King of Kaiju mode in 6 minutes or less

King of Kaiju is a tough nut to crack but there's an easy way to blitz through it. Use Burning Godzilla or Mecha-King Ghidorah as your character, and keep using the Roar + Breath attack to clear each of the six stages in under a minute. Remember to destroy as many buildings as possible, so Godzilla's size increases.

RATCHET & CLANK
EXP CHEAT
An easy trick to ace Challenge Mode

There's an Infinite Ammo cheat in *Ratchet & Clank* that is activated through the main menu, but it disables EXP for your weapon. However, there's a way around this. Select any weapon and note its maximum ammo count. Fire that weapon until it runs out of ammo, then switch the Infinite Ammo cheat on. Fire the weapon the same number of times as its maximum ammo count, then switch Infinite Ammo off again. This will refill your weapon and allow you to gain XP for it. Use this trick to ease the burden of completing Challenge Mode.

GAMER INTERVIEW

THE KING OF TROPHIES

BRIAN ENGLISH
📢 Known for:
PS4Trophies on YouTube

What's your Trophy level, and what's the Gamerscore equivalent?
I have two PSN accounts, one at Trophy level 19 and the other at 34. For Xbox players, that would convert to a Gamerscore of about 293,475.

How many Platinum Trophies have you earned?
Overall, I have earned a total of 188 Platinum Trophies.

What's been your most difficult game to get a Platinum on?
MLB 10 The Show on PS3. This was only earned by .10 percent of the players. What made it exceptionally difficult was the combination of a little skill and a whole lot of luck.

What's been your toughest Trophy unlock?
The most troublesome Trophies I've unlocked were the ten Trophies related to finding all the collectibles in *Uncharted 4*. There were 193 of them. For most people, it's simply a case of following a guide who will walk you through their locations. For me, there was no guide until I made one.

For newcomers, what game is an easy Platinum?

Everyone will tell you Telltale Games make games with the easiest Platinums, such as *Minecraft: Story Mode*. But for me, I recommend *Rocket League*. With a second controller or a friend, it's not difficult and it's a ton of fun.

How many hours a week do you spend unlocking Trophies and making videos?

My days of being a diehard Trophy Hunter are long gone. Running the PS4Trophies YouTube channel has changed my course a bit. When *Uncharted 4* was released on May, 10, 2016, I put in a 120-hour work week playing, recording, and editing the week before launch just so all the

players out there can then Platinum it themselves in 25-30 hours.

If you could pick one retro game to get Trophy support, which game would you choose?

If I had just one wish for a game to come to PlayStation with Trophy support, it would be *The Legend of Zelda: A Link to the Past*.

What's been your most satisfying Trophy unlock to date?

Having unlocked over 10,000 Trophies, my proudest is my first Platinum in *Uncharted: Drake's Fortune* in 2008. At that time, I discovered communities of other gamers who helped me earn Trophies, which then led me to become a YouTuber to help others. There's no friendlier group of gamers in this industry than Trophy hunters. They all work together and help each other achieve a common goal, and that inspires me every day—and that's all thanks to Nathan Drake and his little adventure game.

MASTER ★ SINGLE-PLAYER GAMES!

Who needs to go online when you can play some of the best single-player campaigns ever made? Beat these games alone and become a gaming legend . . .

There are tons of games that are great to play in online multiplayer. But it can be just as much fun to jump into a single-player mode and have the whole virtual playground to yourself. There's nothing wrong with having a few rounds of *Overwatch* or *Rocket League* with your friends, but sometimes you just want to be the only one calling the shots. With all those bad guys to take down, all those quests to compete, and all those scores to beat, playing a solo mode makes everything you do feel like you've really earned it. And you don't need anyone else's help to get there—you're a hero in your own right!

So, we've picked out some of the most exciting single-player games you can play. Plus, we've also ensured you have the best tactics, techniques, and strategies to help you beat even the toughest single-player challenges on offer . . .

THE BIGGEST GAMES

MIRROR'S EDGE CATALYST

One of the best things about playing *Mirror's Edge Catalyst* (apart from just how great the game looks), is the way you can run, leap, slide, and climb your way around a whole city all by yourself.

THE WITNESS

Sometimes all you want to do is wake up on a beautiful sunny island and walk around all day solving puzzles—that's what you get from *The Witness*, and we love it!

DIRT RALLY

Although it's fun to go online and race other players from around the world, nothing beats heading into a single-player career, winning every race, and unlocking every car.

LEGO STAR WARS: THE FORCE AWAKENS

When it comes to playing a single-player campaign, few games come as highly recommended as the LEGO games. The latest one, based on the *Star Wars* movie, even has some extra story missions for you to beat.

RATCHET & CLANK

The new rebooted version of the original *Ratchet & Clank* (which appeared on PS2 way back in 2002) has one of the best single-player stories you can play. It's also full of great races and quests.

UNRAVEL

About a cute little guy made of yarn, the story of *Unravel* is full of surprises, treats, and secrets. It's also got one of the best games that you can play without ever having to go online.

IMPROVE YOUR SKILLS

ESSENTIAL TIP 1

ESSENTIAL TIP 2

TAKE YOUR TIME

Since you're not playing online or in a round of multiplayer, you don't have to rush your way through a level. Take your time, pause when you need a break and beat that story mode or campaign!

DON'T AVOID SIDE MISSIONS

A lot of open-world single-player games feature dozens of side-missions, so don't just stick to the main story. Not only will side-missions give you more things to do, but they'll help you earn new items and XP for leveling up.

ESSENTIAL TIP 3

ESSENTIAL TIP 4

STORY THEN ACHIEVEMENTS

Unless the game tells you otherwise, try and enjoy the story and fun of a game all the way to the end. You can always go back afterward and replay bits to earn Trophies or Achievements once you're done.

DON'T RUN OUT OF CHARGE

Single-player campaigns can be really long. Make sure your controller is fully charged up or filled with new batteries at the start—that way you won't run out of juice mid-game and have to scramble for new ones.

QUICK TRICKS ▶▶▶▶

WHEN IN DOUBT, YOUTUBE IT

Struggling to find a certain treasure or collectible? Why not go online and use a video guide to help you find what you're missing?

KNOW YOUR RARITY

Playing on PS4? Check the rarity on each Trophy to check out how many people have achieved it so far. The rarer it is, the harder it will be to get.

ESSENTIAL TIP 5

ESSENTIAL TIP 6

USE STATS AS A GUIDE

Tons and tons of single-player games have menus and sections that track all your hard work so far (how long you've played for, how many missions you've beaten, etc.). Use stats to help you hit every objective you can!

CUSTOMIZE YOUR CONTROLS

Not every controller layout will suit your playing style. Don't worry though—you can usually head into the options menu and customize different layouts on most games to create a setup that works for you.

ESSENTIAL TIP 7

ESSENTIAL TIP 8

KNOW YOUR DIFFICULTY

Before you start a single-player game, decide what you're playing for. If you're going for Achievements and Trophies, try playing through on a higher difficulty to bag even more by the end of your playthrough.

TAKE A BREAK

Single-player campaigns can be dozens of hours long, but you aren't meant to finish them all in one sitting. Take regular breaks when you reach a save point to give your eyes—and brain!—a rest before heading back in.

BREAK OUT YOUR VITA

Want to continue a single-player game on your PS4, but need to give up the TV? If you have a Vita you can carry on remotely.

USE THE RIGHT CONTROLLER

A normal controller can work for most games, but using special ones (such as steering wheels and fight sticks) might help you play better.

SINGLE-PLAYER ACHIEVEMENTS & TROPHIES

RATCHET & CLANK
MASTER OF WAR

Upgrade every weapon to maximum level

Each weapon in *Ratchet & Clank* has a maximum level of ten, but you'll only be able to reach level five for each one on your first playthrough. Once you've leveled one up to its top level, make sure you switch to a new weapon to get them all at their highest XP level. Then finish a second playthrough in Challenge mode to hit level ten on each gun and bag that silver Trophy.

HARD

MEDIUM

UNRAVEL
OBSESSIVE

Break all the ice on the way to the letterbox in one go

You can get this Achievement in "Chapter Eight: The Letter." There are a total of three rivers and a small puddle in this level, and each one is frozen solid. To bag the 30G this Achievement has to offer you'll need to jump up and down two or three times on each one to make it pop. Just make sure you don't fall in the water once they crack!

MIRROR'S EDGE CATALYST
PRAISE THE RUN

EASY

Reach full Focus and keep it going

Focus is a really important part of playing *Mirror's Edge Catalyst*, as it prevents Faith taking damage from enemies while she's moving. To get this Achievement or Trophy, try going to a quiet area without any bad guys. Now start running in a circle and get your speed up—keep going to maintain full Focus. After about two minutes of constant running, your reward will pop!

THE WITNESS
SHADY TREES

MEDIUM

Activate the Shady Trees laser

The first part of Jonathan Blow's exploration puzzler *The Witness* is all about activating a set of lasers that open up the next area. One of the first lasers you come across is in "Shady Trees," and you'll need to complete a total of 22 puzzles here in order to activate it. Have a pad and pen at hand as you work them out, and pay attention—what you learn in these puzzles will be important later!

DIRT RALLY
SPIRIT OF THE RALLY

Finish an event after heavily damaging three or more components

WRECK NON-IMPORTANT PARTS

2 You need to still finish the event, so don't wreck your wheels, driveshaft, or engine. Instead, damage your radiator, suspension, and exhaust.

CHOOSE THE RIGHT EVENT

1 To get your car smashed up, select a Career Championship event and choose Clubman (giving you six stages to wreck your car).

HARD

Did you know?

Worried you might roll your car while playing *Dirt Rally*? Don't worry, if you roll your rally car and land on your wheels you'll get a Trophy!

START DRIVING LIKE CRAZY

3 In order to damage these less essential parts, try driving off-road to wreck your suspension and hit other cars to break the other two.

LEGO STAR WARS: THE FORCE AWAKENS
UNLEARN WHAT YOU HAVE LEARNED
Rebuild a Multi-build object

EASY

4. NOW BUILD THE OTHER ONE

Once you're done (make sure you've collected whichever collectible you needed with your first build), destroy it with the X or Square button. Now return to where you were before, select the other build option, and the Achievement will be yours!

1. CLEAR THE AREA OF ENEMIES

The LEGO games aren't that hard to finish, but put enough enemies on screen and you'll find yourself being blown to bricky bits. So before trying to build anything, make sure you clear the area of bad guys so you have some time to focus on building.

2. FIND A MULTI-BUILD KIT

These kits have been in the LEGO games since the very first LEGO *Star Wars* game back in 2005, and form a huge part of your virtual LEGO experience. You'll know them by the pieces of LEGO that jump around on the floor.

3. BUILD THE FIRST MULTI-BUILD

Head on over to the collection of bricks hopping on the floor and hold the B or Circle button to start building an object. Use the left analogue stick to select which of the red-outlined structures to build.

LEGO MARVEL'S AVENGERS
YOU ASKED FOR IT
Stop 10 random crimes in Manhattan during a single session

While you're roaming the open-world hub of Manhattan, Agent Coulson will call you and let you know there's a crime being committed nearby. The scene of the crime will now appear on your minimap, so head over there as quick as you can and stop the bad guys in their tracks. Do this ten times in a row and that 50G will be yours!

SKYLANDERS SUPERCHARGERS
EON'S ELITE

HARD

Complete Story Mode on Nightmare difficulty

Nightmare is the highest difficulty in *Skylanders SuperChargers*, so you'll need to play a little differently to get this gold Trophy to pop. For a start, fight only when you have to (to open gates, defeat bosses, etc.). Otherwise, just run past enemies and hang onto as much health as you can!

MEDIUM

MEDIUM

ORI AND THE BLIND FOREST: DEFINITIVE EDITION
DEADLY DASH
Kill five enemies with Charge Jump

UNLOCK THE MOVE

1 To start, you'll need to head over to Sorrow Pass and unlock the Charge Jump. To perform the move, hold down LT and press A to jump.

FIND A CLUMP OF ENEMIES

2 You'll need to take out five enemies at once. Try breaking one of those pink blob bad guys into lots of little blobs . . .

LET THEM GATHER AROUND YOU . . .

3 . . . then boom! You'll have to take a few hits to begin with, but once the enemies are all around you, use your dash and five of them should be defeated.

GUITAR HERO LIVE
POINTDEXTER
MEDIUM

Score 100,000,000 points in GHTV

Don't worry, you don't need to score 100,000,000 points in one session—that would be crazy! This one builds up over time, so the game will remember how many points you've banked since you first played GHTV mode. The best way to maximize your point haul is to play at the highest difficulty you're comfortable with, upgrade your guitar, and use Hero Powers wisely.

Did you know?

There are over 200 heroes and villains to unlock and play as in LEGO *Avengers*. Collect those studs so you can afford them all.

WORLD OF TANKS

World of Tanks is explosive—literally. But there's much more to this multiplayer shooter than initially appears. Yes, there's lots of blowing stuff up, but at its core, *World of Tanks* is a game of tactical positioning and team strategy.

TIPS & STRATEGY

BEGINNER
THE RIGHT TANK

Pick the right tank for the job. Light tanks, for example, are best used as scouts—the idea is to spot the enemy and then get away quickly.

HUNT IN PACKS

Driving off on your own at the start of a match is a rookie mistake. Stick with your teammates for strength in numbers instead.

INTERMEDIATE
STAY COVERED

Try to stay hidden when possible. Reducing the profile of your tank by staying under cover makes you both harder to spot and harder to hit.

THE HIGHER GROUND

High ground gives you the advantage. An enemy coming over the top of a hill won't be able to get their gun low enough to shoot you when moving, but you can hit them.

ADVANCED
FLANKED

The sides, or flanks, are the most vulnerable part of a tank. Learn to adjust your position in battle to protect them from the enemy.

TRACKING

Aim for a tank's tracks and you can leave it unable to move, making it a sitting duck that you and your teammates can easily take down.

CHEATS & SECRETS

REPORT CHEATERS

On the PC version you might encounter gamers who use cheats to always hit you. This isn't fair, so report them.

PUSH THE BUTTON

On the map Komarin, there is a skeleton holding a button, hidden in the lake. What the button does is still a mystery . . .

TOP 4 Achievements & Trophies

⬌ TOUGHEST ACHIEVEMENT
WAR
Destroy 500 tanks. MP only

Destroying 500 tanks in a game about tanks isn't as easy as it seems. Your best strategy is to focus on unlocking heavy tanks. The more power, the easier it is to beat the opposition.

☑ EASIEST ACHIEVEMENT
NEW TOY
Acquire a tank upgrade

Once you've played a few matches, you'll have more than enough Silver to unlock this one. Simply access the garage for one of your light tanks, then buy the cheapest upgrade available.

☺ WEIRDEST TROPHY
DEATH FROM ABOVE
Land on or drive over an enemy, killing them. MP only

Shoot the dummy tank in training mode in the side and nudge it to the swamp. When it starts to roll down a hill, drive on top of the dummy and this Trophy will be yours.

😎 COOLEST TROPHY
VICTORY!
Survive, and win a battle. MP only

Work as a team to help to spot and take down enemies, and defend your position. With all your newly found *World of Tanks* knowledge, "Victory!" certainly won't be your last Trophy

OVERCOOKED

In this frantic cooking game, you work in a team of up to four players to prepare, cook, and serve up a variety of tasty treats for customers. It's a perfect balance of total chaos and streamlined skill.

TIPS & STRATEGY

BEGINNER
BEST WITH FRIENDS

You *can* play *Overcooked* in single-player, but it's a game that's clearly designed to be played with friends. So grab some buddies to get the best out of it.

KEEP TALKING

Communication is key in *Overcooked*, so keep chatting with your friends to make sure you are working together.

INTERMEDIATE
DIVIDE TASKS

You shouldn't all be tripping over each other trying to do the same thing. Divide up your culinary responsibilities so you each have your own task.

BE EFFICIENT

Taking a veggie over to a friend, getting them to chop it, and then taking it back to the pot is quicker than one person doing it all alone.

ADVANCED
EXPERIMENT

If you want to get those three-star ratings, you need to experiment with different strategies to find ways to deliver more orders.

FIRE FIGHTING

Overcooked's final boss will shoot fireballs that set your kitchen on fire, so you should make sure you've had some practice with the fire extinguisher beforehand.

CHEATS & SECRETS

FUN WITH FOUR

You don't need four controllers for four-player *Overcooked*. There's a mode that lets two players share a controller.

KEEP A COOL HEAD

The fireballs thrown out by the last boss have a random element, so don't feel bad about restarting if you've taken some unlucky hits.

TOP 4
Achievements & Trophies

☑ EASIEST ACHIEVEMENT
LETTUCE BEGIN
Deliver a recipe to the Great and Terrifying Ever Peckish

It doesn't get much easier than this wonderful palate cleanser. Start preparing salads for the meatball monster and you'll obtain this as soon as you deliver the first one correctly.

☺ TOUGHEST TROPHY
ALL THE TRIMMINGS
Be awarded three stars in every kitchen

Without question the most difficult Trophy in the game. Best done in co-op, you need to utilize your time masterfully to keep ingredients and utensils on the move.

⬌ MULTIPLAYER TROPHY
DOES NOT PLAY WELL WITH OTHERS
Complete a kitchen in versus mode

Overcooked is usually best played in co-op, but sometimes there's nothing like taking on your pals in the kitchen. Remember, staying calm is the key to success.

☺ WEIRDEST ACHIEVEMENT
OVERCOOKED
Extinguish a burning kitchen

If you let any food overcook or boil over, it'll burst into flames. Grab the fire extinguisher, brave the heat, and do your best to put out the flames. This is a reward for failing at the game, but saving your kitchen!

TRANSFORMERS: DEVASTATION

No developer does action games as well as PlatinumGames, and *Devastation* is every bit as good as fans would hope. Its fast-paced combat system has an amazing degree of depth, and every character plays completely differently.

TIPS & STRATEGY

BEGINNER
START OUT EASY

Work your way up through the difficulty levels rather than jumping in high—you'll get better weapons to make your life easier this way.

AUTOBOT ALLIES

Focus your attention on one character over the course of each run. They'll level up faster and get better gear than if you switch between them.

INTERMEDIATE
DODGE OFFSET

As in Platinum's other action games, combos can be continued after dodges by holding the attack button down while evading.

USE YOUR GUNS

They feel quite weak at first, but guns can be a great way of opening up enemies for big attacks or dealing with them from a safe distance.

ADVANCED
MASTER DODGING

Once you learn each enemy's attack patterns, it's possible to finish the game without taking a hit. Perfect dodges also lead to powerful counterattacks.

WEAK WEAPONS WIN

If you're good enough to get through fights with underpowered gear, you'll be able to land more hits and score much higher than by just one-shotting everything!

CHEATS & SECRETS

PLAY AS GRIMLOCK

The Dinobot leader isn't unlocked from the start. You'll need to beat Chapter Two before you can use him.

MAKE IT HARDER

Beat the game to unlock the punishing Magnus difficulty, then battle through that to get Prime mode.

TOP 3
Achievements & Trophies

☑ EASIEST ACHIEVEMENT
FULL THROTTLE
Defeated 100 enemies with Vehicle/Dino Attacks

This is far easier than it sounds and easy to pick up while playing through the campaign. To be safe, use a hammer weapon, since this will result in two vehicle attacks per combo.

🎯 COOLEST ACHIEVEMENT
URBAN LANDSCAPING
Knock Devastator into a building three times

On "Commander," lure Devastator near a building, drop it to its knees with a counter, climb its leg, and perform a vehicle attack into its chest.

🏆 SECRET TROPHY
FLYSWATTER
Finish the lift battle in Chapter 2 without taking damage from Insecticons

Pay close attention to where the Insecticons are spawning. Playing on a lower difficulty helps to make them drop faster, but once you come to the big Insecticon, memorize its attacks and be ready to launch a focus dodge.

THE EXPERT SAYS . . .

SOOO MUNGRY
YouTuber and Transformers fan

Your main focus should be to stay alive, so that means you should dodge a ton, but at the same time you want to make sure you are stringing combos together for maximum damage.

UNRAVEL

This awesome puzzle platformer might be cute and whimsical, but it requires a lot of patience and ingenuity to truly master. Take the time to learn the ropes when it comes to Yarny's skill set, though, and you'll be fine.

TIPS & STRATEGY

BEGINNER ◄
UNRAVELING

Yarny unravels as you move forward, so keep an eye out for string to refill. Use your lasso to move objects and find hidden string.

GET CREATIVE

Many of Unravel's puzzles have multiple solutions, so don't be afraid to experiment! You can always retrace your steps by reeling yarn back in.

INTERMEDIATE ◄◄
DISTRACT CRABS

Crabs can be a hazard for poor Yarny, so you'll want to distract them. Use yarn to pull oysters toward crabs to grab their attention.

BUILD A BRIDGE

You'll find making yarn bridges really useful for solving puzzles. You can also slingshot yourself off bridges by holding Down on the controller.

ADVANCED ◄◄◄
NO BACKTRACKING

Tying yourself to a checkpoint usually means you can't backtrack, so explore the previous area first if you're hunting down all collectibles.

PERFECTION

If you're going for a perfect Gold Crown run, you can reload a previous checkpoint when you're in danger without it counting as a failure.

HEATS & SECRETS

FIVE TO FIND

There are five secrets to be found in every level. However, Level 11 has two parts, and there are none in the first part of the stage.

CAPTAIN HOOK

Watch out for hooks that seem to make no sense. If you can't figure out why they are there, they are probably hiding a secret!

TOP 4 Achievements & Trophies

UNRAVEL

⬌ TOUGHEST ACHIEVEMENT
NOT SO FRAGILE AFTER ALL
Finish each level from start to finish without dying

To pull off this grueling feat, you'll to need to remember each pitfall. Then, play through the level again, taking extra care not to die.

◉ COOLEST ACHIEVEMENT
PATHFINDER
Make it to the water wheel without using a log raft

After the first bridge in "Chapter 5," you'll come across a section where you are supposed to use a log raft. However, with some skilled platforming, you can prove that you don't need it!

❀ SECRET TROPHY
PACIFIST
Make it through the mire without swatting mosquitos

In "Chapter 3: Berry Mire," as you reach the rock face going down, followed by a water section, don't use your lasso in case you accidentally hit a mosquito. Instead, walk up to objects and tie yarn onto them to pull them around and get through this section.

☑ EASIEST TROPHY
MISSING PIECE
Find the first missing piece

Just finish the first chapter! The trickiest part is where Yarny needs to jump a gate. Go back to find the tricycle, lasso it, and pull it to the gate to use it as a climbing frame.

QUICK TIPS & TRICKS

RATCHET & CLANK

You can throw the pulsing Proton Drum weapon into a group of enemies—or at a boss—and it will do damage with each pulse. Upgrade it as much as you can, then throw it first in boss fights. This will sap the boss's health right away, before you even start attacking with your other weapons!

SKYLANDERS

The toys-to-life genre has exploded in the last few years, and it's largely thanks to *Skylanders*! The series introduces cool new concepts and mechanics with every release, so you never know what the team might do next . . .

TIPS & STRATEGY

BEGINNER
USE OLD FRIENDS

If you've played a *Skylanders* game before, your heroes will still be leveled up when you use them in a new game—a great way to get an early boost.

AMASS AN ARMY

With just a few Skylanders, harder levels might give you trouble. The more you collect, the more chances you have before needing to restart.

INTERMEDIATE
CO-OP RICHES

Get a friend to join you in co-op and you'll both get the rewards—treasure is awarded to both active Skylanders, so you'll both be rolling in gold!

KARDS WITH KAOS

After beating the game, you can play Skystones against returning villain, Kaos. You can get rewards once per day, so just keep challenging him.

ADVANCED
GETTING HUNGRY?

Rather than letting your most powerful Skylanders faint, pull them out before that happens, then tag them back in to grab healing items you find later.

WHAT A NIGHTMARE

Super-tough Nightmare difficulty is back and once again, there's a Trophy tied to beating it. You'll need a huge collection of Skylanders to get through the last boss . . .

CHEATS & SECRETS

INFINITE CASH

Place breakable treasures near Persephone in the hub. Smash them with an Elite, quickly talk to her, and repeat!

POWER LEVELING

Head to "Battle Brawl Island" in *SuperChargers* to level up. There are loads of enemies so you'll grow strong quickly.

☑ EASIEST ACHIEVEMENT
READY TO ROLL

Equip your first Mod

Skylanders SuperChargers is all about modding your vehicle by switching out your boosters, tires, and so on, to improve its performance. Simply equip any mod and "Ready To Roll" is yours.

🎒 SECRET ACHIEVEMENT
LIGHT GIVER

Defeat The Darkness on any difficulty in the game

Drive through the yellow rings to power up your vehicle and boost into The Darkness. This will stun him. Do as much damage as you can while he is stunned and then repeat.

👥 CO-OP TROPHY
ROAD TRIP

Enter a vehicle in the Co-Op mode

It's incredibly fun playing *Skylanders* with a friend, better still when you start enjoying the vehicles together. Simply jump in a Barrel Blaster or Gold Rusher with a buddy and there you go—you've got a Trophy.

😄 FUNNIEST TROPHY
HORN HONKER

Honk your first vehicle horn

If you honk your horn as soon as you get in your first SuperCharger by clicking in the left stick, you will be rewarded with this Trophy. That's all you have to do. For some reason, honking a horn is always funny.

OVERWATCH

Blizzard's competitive shooter is one of the best on the market. It's simple to pick up and play, yet offers a level of depth that allows for real mastery of each character, as seen in the game's impact on the eSports scene.

TIPS & STRATEGY

BEGINNER
TAKE IT EASY

When learning the game, don't bother with tricky Heroes like Zenyatta or Symmetra. Stick to easier characters, like Soldier: 76 and Reaper, until you're comfortable with the game.

INTERMEDIATE
LEARN TO INTERRUPT

Many Ultimate abilities can be shut down by skills like McCree's flashbang, Roadhog's chain, and Ana's sleep dart. Be ready to react.

LISTEN WELL

Sounds from enemies are significantly louder than from allies, helping you get a better idea of who is coming and from where. There are also other audio hints, such as an enemy Mercy speaking German when using abilities.

REACH NEW HEIGHTS

Some characters have easy ways to reach high ground but others can improvise—Mei's ice wall can give her or her allies a boost while Junkrat can get air from his own remote mines.

ADVANCED
RIGHT BACK AT YA!

Genji's deflection skill is deadly in the right hands. It ruins over-eager Bastion players, for instance, and can even deflect a good number of Ultimate abilities.

HEATS & SECRETS

MURLOC MADNESS

In Hanamura, there's a shop called Rikimaru, and the mascot is a Murloc from *WoW*. It gurgles when you shoot it!

ANYONE FOR CARDS?

Hearthstone seems pretty popular in *Overwatch*—tablets running Blizzard's card game can be found on three maps.

TOUGHEST ACHIEVEMENT
RAPID DISCORD
Get four kills or assists with Zenyatta's Orb of Discord within six seconds

Teamwork makes this easier. Have Zarya use her Graviton Surge, then another teammate use a damaging Ultimate ability, while you use Orb of Discord to grab assists.

EASIEST TROPHY
HUGE SUCCESS
Teleport 20 players in a single game as Symmetra

It seems difficult, but there's a simple trick to it. Just place your own teleporter in the spawn room and teleport yourself. You can teleport six times before you need a fresh teleporter, so four teleporters will do the job.

COOLEST ACHIEVEMENT
SLICE AND DICE
Kill 4 enemies with a single use of Genji's Dragonblade

Eliminate someone with Genji's Swift Strike and you can use it again right away. Use this when Dragonblade is active to quickly tear through an enemy team.

MASTER MEI'S SKILLS

1. BEWARE THE WALL

The difference between good and great players is ice wall use. Throw up walls to divide the enemy and target stragglers, or to defend against enemy Ultimates.

2. SHIELD YOURSELF

If you run into trouble, you can freeze yourself in place and heal over time. Most players will attack you as soon as you come out of the ice block, so throw up a wall to stay safe.

3. EVERYBODY FREEZE

Mei's Ultimate covers an area with a blizzard, freezing anyone in it. Use it to scare panicked players away from the objective or the payload, splitting them up so you can pick them off.

4. SNEAK FROM THE SIDES

Mei's best position is attacking teams from the sides, where she can get close and freeze them before they have a chance to react.

I AM YOUR SHIELD
Block 8,000 Damage with Reinhardt's Barrier Shield without dying

TEAM COMPOSITION MATTERS

1 This works best when defending an objective or the payload. You need at least one Bastion or Torbjorn on your team, and a Support player, like Mercy, who can heal you.

SET UP THE TEAM

2 Use your Barrier Shield in front of Bastion or Torbjorn's turret. This is an extremely aggressive way to defend against the attacking team and your shield will draw all the fire.

TOP TORBJORN TIPS

1. DEFEND FOR YOUR LIFE

The easiest way to get a 20-player streak is on a Defend map with Torbjorn. Set a turret up in a corner to shield it from teams trying to capture the final point.

2. FIRE AWAY

Your gun has a decent long-range shot, so use it to chip away at the enemy's health as they approach the defend point. Don't risk a shot from up close, unless you have to!

3. LOOK AFTER THE TURRET

Keep an eye on your turret health and fix it between enemy attacks. Don't try and fix it while it's being attacked though, as this is a huge risk to take. Clear out the attackers first.

4. MOLTEN COOOORE

Torbjorn's Ultimate doesn't just power him up but his turret as well. Save it for when your turret is about to be destroyed or if the defend point is being overrun.

RETREAT . . . THEN RETURN

3 You can soak up 2,000 damage before your shield shatters and you need to recharge. You might want to consider recharging before that, though. Do it during breaks in the action.

BACK AWAY . . .

4 If the enemy manages to get behind your shield and the turret, break away from the action and regroup. Keep blocking damage until you hit 8,000 to get the Trophy.

BATTLEBORN

This energetic, colorful shooter is a blend of multiplayer online battle arena and first-person shooter. Its cool characters each have unique abilities that include conjuring powerful geysers and throwing spore sacks!

TIPS & STRATEGY

BEGINNER ◄
PLAY THE CAMPAIGN

Playing against AI in *Battleborn*'s campaign will ease you into the game and help you learn how it works before you head into online modes.

CHOOSE WISELY

Test out the different heroes available for you to choose from to get an idea of how they work and find which one suits your playstyle best.

INTERMEDIATE ◄◄
SHARD SPENDER

Keep an eye out for glowing yellow shards dotted around the map. Use them to build and upgrade turrets and other defenses to help your team.

RETREAT!

Taking out enemies is a big boost to in-game XP, so you don't want to let your foes get that advantage. Retreat when things are looking bad.

ADVANCED ◄◄◄
GO TEAM!

Working as a team is key to success. If you push towards the objectives as a unit, rather than solo, you've got a much better chance of taking them.

DO YOUR RESEARCH

Knowledge is power. Head to the *Battleborn* website to read all about every character's strengths, weaknesses, and abilities, then take your knowledge into battle.

CHEATS & SECRETS

ACCESS DENIED

Keep trying to access the locked Gear Bank before hitting rank 3 to be treated to some funny dialogue.

UNLOCK AMBRA

To unlock Ambra, either reach rank fourteen, or win five matches with a Jennerit character.

🏆 SECRET ACHIEVEMENT
A TYRANT UNDONE
Defeat Rendain

For this challenge, complete "Episode 8: The Heliophage." It's the last level in *Battleborn* and you face off against Rendain. It's a long, difficult battle, so get ready!

👁 COOLEST TROPHY
GOTTA PUNCH 'EM ALL
Land a killing blow on each Battleborn at least once

Landing a finishing blow on every Battleborn won't only let everyone know that you're an awesome player, it'll earn you this Trophy too!

☑ EASIEST ACHIEVEMENT
DIVIDE BY ZERO HOUR
Complete The Algorithm on any difficulty

Take a team of friends along with you and set the difficulty to Easy and you should breeze through the game's first campaign mission.

👥 MULTIPLAYER TROPHY
WHEN YOU ROLL UP WITH THE SQUAD LIKE
Enter matchmaking with a full team of 5 players

You don't have to find a game to get this Trophy. Just set up a party with four friends and enter matchmaking together.

GAMER INTERVIEW

GAMER INTERVIEW

ONE OF *THE* GAMERSCORE LEADERS

REDMPTIONDENIED

📢 Known for:
1 million Gamerscore milestone

What do you think is key to a good Gamerscore? Is it time, skill, or something else?

Time is the biggest factor, but I would say mindset is equally as important. Certain Achievements definitely require a high level of skill, but scoring a lot of points involves focusing on the easiest and quickest games out there. I'd say I'm at least competent at most games, but wouldn't say I'm especially skilled in any genre in particular, because of how much I jump around games.

What games have you played purely for Achievements, only for you to be surprised by how much you enjoyed the game itself?

Off the top of my head I'd say *Shovel Knight*, an indie platformer. *Ori and the Blind Forest*, another platformer, is one of my favorite games on the Xbox One. It's also the game that I was playing when I hit a million Gamerscore. *Steamworld Dig* was another fairly basic concept but something I really enjoyed for what it was. Also, *Adventures of Pip* was another indie title I really liked.

RedmptionDenied
Last seen: Home (Xbox One)
3 hours ago
⊕ 1,051,454

Reputation
Good player

Send message

Compare games

Add friend

Ori and the Blind Forest has won many fans with its brilliant platforming and art style.

Although it takes only a few hours to complete, *Steamworld Dig* is a lot of fun and comes highly recommended by most Achievement hunters.

Shovel Knight has won over players thanks to its well-designed levels and smart humor.

What was the least enjoyable game you've played through for Achievements?

It's hard to just pick one as there have been quite a few very terrible games along the way. The Kinect stuff probably stands out, if only for the embarrassment factor. There's no real way to explain to a "serious" gamer why exactly you're playing titles such as *Let's Cheer* or *Alvin and the Chipmunks: Chipwrecked*! Other than Kinect I'd probably put *Brave: A Warrior's Tale* up there, as well as *Soda Drinker Pro* and *Divekick*.

Are there any types of Achievements you hate trying to unlock?

I think I can speak for the entire Achievement community when I say anything that's completely luck-based. We hate those with a passion. The most recent example was an update for *Rocket League* where you needed two particular items that

could only be won through online games. It was 100 percent luck-based if you got them. Some people would get them within a day, others have played for weeks and still nothing. At least in that case the game itself is very fun to play, but still, a game that you can play for hours without being able to improve your chances of success is very frustrating.

What sort of responses do you get online to your Gamerscore?

Honestly I don't get that many random messages on Xbox Live. What I do get is mostly positive, but of course you always get a few random negative people. I just block them and move along with my day. I don't expect the vast majority of people to understand what I do. All I can say is everyone should have a hobby. This is mine and I take it more passionately than most.

40 NOTE STREAK

GUITAR HERO LIVE

It's *Guitar Hero*, but not as you know it. The old five-key guitar is gone, replaced with a shiny new six-button one. That means even experts will have to learn how to rock all over again in this rhythm-action title.

TIPS & STRATEGY

BEGINNER
SPOTTING PATTERNS

Once you've got a feel for the new guitar, try practicing chord shapes and hand placements. That muscle memory will make it far easier to hit those chords when they come up.

SAVE YOUR PLAYS

If you want to play any of the on-disc songs, do it in the Live mode—otherwise, launching them from GHTV mode will cost you a Play each time, and that's just a waste.

INTERMEDIATE
NO NEED TO STRUM

Some notes have different borders than usual—these can be played without

strumming so long as you hit the previous note. These are known by pro players as hammer-ons and pull-offs.

CHANGING CHANNEL

When playing songs live on the GHTV streams, don't be afraid to switch between channels. Just be sure to do it after a song ends so you don't miss out on the rewards!

ADVANCED
LITTLE HIGH, LITTLE LOW

Just like on a real guitar, it's possible to press down additional notes below the one being played without being penalized. Use this for sequences of rapidly changing notes, such as solos.

CHEATS & SECRETS

TRY NEW SONGS

Tracks are added to special Premium Shows before they go into rotation on the regular GHTV list.

36 NOTE STREAK

THE REAL DEAL

Bands in *GH Live* aren't real, but all performers are actual musicians and appear under their real names.

COOLEST TROPHY
AMAZING!
Earn a 1,000 note streak in GHTV mode

Cry of Achilles by Alter Bridge is the best track to get this streak on, since there are over 1,000 notes on Regular difficulty. A perfect run will see you earn you the Trophy.

WEIRDEST ACHIEVEMENT
CREDIT IS DUE
Watch the credits. Twice.

Considering how much skill is required to get the other Achievements, this one is a little bit odd. After playing the last show of the Live segment, select and watch the credits twice. It takes about 45 minutes!

SECRET ACHIEVEMENT
DO IT YOU WON'T DO IT
Switch the crowd from negative to positive in the last seconds

When the song's almost over, stop playing to lose crowd favor. Then, with 20 or so seconds left, hit every note so the crowd goes wild again.

TOUGHEST TROPHY
OOOOH, YOU FANCY
Get 100 percent in four songs on Expert difficulty

Keep playing songs until you're good enough. One clever time save: it doesn't say *different* songs. Master one, then just play it perfectly three more times.

ROCK BAND 4

ROCK BAND 4

Not content with giving the world the gift of music with the *Guitar Hero* series, developer Harmonix went one louder with *Rock Band*. Play solo or bring in friends to form a band for the ultimate rhythm-action game experience.

TIPS & STRATEGY

BEGINNER ◄
COORDINATION IS KEY

When playing multiplayer, every player should aim to activate Overdrive at the same time for the best score multiplier. Follow the drummer's lead, since they can only trigger their ability after a "fill" section in their track.

GET CALIBRATED

Most HDTVs have a degree of input lag, which can make the audio fall out of sync with the note chart. This can really affect your timing when you're trying to perfect tracks, so run the calibration tool from the menu before you hit the road with your new band.

INTERMEDIATE ◄◄
KNOW YOUR ROLE

If you're looking to improve, specialize in one instrument. While it's fun to play a little bit of everything, you won't improve as quickly that way.

BASH BUTTONS

Drummers, take note— during a "Big Rock Ending" or "Freestyle Fill," hit the controller button as well as the drums for massive points.

ADVANCED ◄◄◄
GOING FOR GOLD

There's a secret rating above five Stars. Complete any song near-perfectly and you'll be upgraded to five Gold Stars for your efforts.

CHEATS & SECRETS

OVERFLOWING OVERDRIVE

Struggling with this Trophy? Play *Dead Black* on Hard and activate Overdrive along with the vocals after the second slow section.

NO FAIL MODE

Jump into the options and enable this option. It will allow you to play and learn songs on harder difficulties.

🎙 MULTIPLAYER ACHIEVEMENT

PITCH SESSION

Earn a Triple Awesome rating on Vocal Harmonies

You need three microphones and three good singers to get this one. When you all know a song well enough, you should be able to hit at least *one* Triple Awesome.

⬌ HARDEST ACHIEVEMENT

ROCK BAND IMMORTAL

Earn 5 Stars on every song on Expert in Quickplay mode

You can mix and match instruments, just so long as you get top honors on every on-disc track.

😄 FUNNIEST TROPHY

I TOLD YOU I HATED THIS ONE

As a Singer, fail out of a song you voted against

Completed in multiplayer (where you can vote on songs), this is easily achieved. Just make sure you get a song you definitely can't sing and then reap the rewards of your tuneless wailing!

😎 COOLEST TROPHY

ALL TAPPED OUT

Play a Freestyle Guitar Solo composed of at least 80 percent tapping

It's easy enough to use only tapping during a solo, so ignore any prompts, strike your best rock pose, and tap away until this pops for you!

WWE 2K16

Whether you choose to relive Stone Cold Steve Austin's most famous moments in the 2K Showcase, or make some new ones with your own wrestler creation in the game's cool career mode, you'd better get ready to rumble.

TIPS & STRATEGY

BEGINNER ◄
CHAIN WRESTLING

In the chain wrestling mini-game you get early on in matches, move your stick to find the sweet spot where the controller vibrates and hold it there to gain control.

IT'S NOT CHEATING

Pay attention to the match rules. If "No Disqualification" is active, you can grab a weapon from underneath the ring.

INTERMEDIATE ◄◄
PUNISH THEM

If you're playing a friend, pay attention to their Reversal counter. If it's empty, it's time to hit some big moves. They can't do anything about it!

SIZE MATTERS

When creating a wrestler, think about the style you want to have. A 7-ft giant won't fit a high-flying style, as their agility will be limited.

ADVANCED ◄◄◄
REVERSAL MASTER

The Reversal icon pops up so quickly that you're better off getting a feel for the timing of Reversals so you can just hit the Reversal button at the right moment instinctively.

RING GENERAL

Each move damages a different part of the body. Focus on one to weaken an opponent for a submission that targets that body part.

CHEATS & ►►► SECRETS

HIGH FLYING

If you hold down the finisher button when performing top rope finishers, the wrestler will stand up until you release it.

CROWD FAVORITE

A glitch lets you "Strong Irish Whip" opponents into the crowd in the corner above the announcers' table.

🔄 FUNNIEST ACHIEVEMENT
OH! MY!
Put your opponent through a table using an OMG Moment

Stand near the commentary table. Irish Whip your opponent onto the table then climb the turnbuckle. When you see the OMG prompt, hit your finisher button.

☑ COOLEST ACHIEVEMENT
OVER THE ROPES YOU GO
Eliminate 12 opponents using the same superstar in a single Royal Rumble match

Always keep one finisher stored so you can escape if someone is trying to push you over. Strong Irish Whips and corner grapples are the key to eliminating opponents.

🏆 TOUGHEST TROPHY
DON'T TRUST ANYBODY
Complete all objectives in 2K Showcase mode

These are easier if you soften up your opponents first. So, once you reach a point where you're ready to get a pin, pick them back up and start crossing off objectives. If you miss any, you can always go back and replay the matches.

🏆 RAREST TROPHY
SUPLEX CITY
With Brock Lesnar, execute German Suplex 4 or Back Suplex 2 ten times in a single match

When behind your opponent, with their back to you, press the left stick towards them and then either A if you're on the Xbox or X on the PS4. For the back suplex, hold the button down instead of just tapping it to pull it off. Bang! That's gotta hurt.

QUICK TIPS & TRICKS

ROCKET LEAGUE

You can actually blow up cars on the opposing team to take them out of the game for a few seconds. Fill your boost bar and hold down the boost button to accelerate as much as you can. When you're at full speed, aim at an opponent and drive right into them to make them explode! While they wait to respawn, you can take advantage of the opposition team's reduced numbers to try and score.

INDIE TIPS & TRICKS

GAMES THAT STAND OUT FROM THE CROWD

Most of the biggest games out there, such as *Overwatch*, *FIFA*, and *Final Fantasy*, are made by big-name developers, with huge development teams. However, in recent years, a number of independent or "indie" games, made by much smaller teams, have started to make a name for themselves. These games are usually totally unique, with interesting gameplay styles, old-school graphics, and crazy plot lines. Unique as they are, when it comes to quality, they are every bit as good as the big-budget blockbusters made by the world's biggest studios. Give them a try yourself to find out—armed with our expert tips to help guide you through even the most challenging indie titles.

SUPERHOT
BUY SOME TIME

Stunning your enemies

When you run out of ammo in the slo-mo shooter *Superhot*, it doesn't mean your weapon is useless. You can actually throw it at an enemy to stun them, buying you some time and sometimes even making them drop their weapon.

VELOCITY 2X
SPEED DEMON

Beat your friends' best times

There's a trick you can use to get some insanely fast times in *Velocity 2X*. The effect of speed boost pads is cumulative, so if you place a teleporter just before a speed pad, and keep teleporting back to it, you can rev your ship's speed up to incredible levels. Now you just have to learn to control your ship at those crazy high speeds!

ENTER THE GUNGEON
BUILD THE BULLET

How to unlock the game's secret endings

1. FIRST BULLET PART: PRIME PRIMER

Getting all four parts of the bullet will unlock the secret endings. Buy the first part in the shop for 110 shells.

2. SECOND BULLET PART: ARCANE GUNPOWDER

In "Chamber 3," dodge roll from minecart to minecart to reach the Arcane Gunpowder.

3. THIRD BULLET PART: PLANAR LEAD

In "Chamber 4," there's a large room that seems to be empty but an invisible pathway is shown with any weapon that leaves a trail. Follow the path.

4. FOURTH BULLET PART: OBSIDIAN SHELL CASING

In "Chamber 5," after defeating the boss all you have to do is destroy the skull to find the Obsidian Shell Casing.

SHOVEL KNIGHT
NICE HAT . . .

Unlock the secret boss Mr. Hat

You need to unlock "Armor Outpost" by beating the "Iron Whale" area. Once you've unlocked "Armor Outpost," go there and head all the way over to the left to find the fancy hat and dress shop. The three "moochers" in there want 1,000 Gold each. Hand over the Gold and they will leave. The owner of the shop, Mr. Hat, will then appear and fight you for your helmet.

AXIOM VERGE
SECRET WORLDS

Searching for hidden doors

Finding secret worlds can be tough, since they never appear in the same place in each playthrough. Try to walk or teleport through every wall that's three blocks high and check your health bar. It will have very subtle scan lines running through it as you approach if a secret world entrance is there. Then just step through to discover it.

DEFENSE GRID 2
KNOW YOUR TOWERS

How to be the ultimate defender

Make sure you have a good mix of towers tailored to the challenges you are facing in *Defense Grid 2*. The Laser tower is great against fast enemies, for example. Tower placement is also important—you should place the slow firing Cannon in key places where it can hit enemies over a wide range.

LIFELESS PLANET
POWER UP

Just what are those glowing green rocks?

When you are playing Lifeless Planet, you will come across some glowing green relics and rocks. Take the rocks over to the relic and place it in front of it. You can then activate a claw that comes out of the back of your suit to pick up the rock and place it in the hole in the middle of the relic. This will power it up.

Kali accepts your sacrifice!
She bestows a gift upon you!

SPELUNKY
RESTORE YOUR HEALTH
Win the kapala from Kali

There's an easy, but not very nice, way to get this useful health-restoring item. Have a second player join you in co-op and make sure the second player carries any damsel you save. When you find a Kali shrine, sacrifice the damsel and the second player to get the kapala.

15:23 - Work (Day 10)

THE ESCAPISTS
GRAY MATTERS
Boost your intellect

The easiest way to build your intellect in this prison escape game is—weirdly—with memes on the Internet in the starting prison. Just LOL at the cats on the computer whenever you have a spare moment and your intellect will skyrocket. Other prisons have books, which you can also read to build your intellect.

Dental Floss
[Component]

STEAMWORLD DIG
BECOME A MINING MASTER
Four tips to help you survive and thrive underground

1. GREED IS BAD
Make sure you don't get too greedy. If you get splatted by a boulder or taken out by an enemy, you will respawn back in town, but it will cost you half of your mined gold! Spend your gold before that happens instead.

2. DIGGING DEEP
More valuable loot and resources can be found the deeper you dig. Teleporters are useful for these deep mining trips, allowing you to quickly return to higher ground if you find yourself in danger.

CHARIOT
SPEEDRUNNING
Get gold medals
To finish each level quick enough to get a gold medal, make the most of your chariot on flat ground. Get some distance between you and the chariot, attach your rope, then wind up while working. The chariot will gain more speed than you, so you can hop aboard to take advantage.

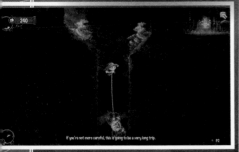

CASTLESTORM— DEFINITIVE EDITION
HARD AS ROCK
A special strategy for defeating the giant stone golem . . .
When taking on the stone golem, you need to hit his glowing green eyes when he raises a rock above his head. This will stun the golem. Use this opportunity to teleport your hero onto the battlefield and attack it.

BEACH BUGGY RACING
BEAT THE BOSS
How to get the car you need
When you first get to the boss race, you might find yourself struggling. If that's the case, simply return to earlier races to earn some extra coins, then use that cash to get the fast car you need to allow you to keep up with the boss and finally beat them.

PONCHO
THE CASSEROLE HAMSTER
Hear a secret song

Pick the "Through The Caves" level and in the far back plane of the level, slightly to the right, you can stomp through the ground to a cave. In the cave, head to the right and activate the device you find there. A dancing hamster will appear and you will be treated to a funny little song about making a casserole.

3. MAKE A SHORTCUT
Dig straight down from the entrance to get to your mining area. You can then use this shaft to wall jump up and slide down to make your trips quicker.

4. STAY QUIET
You can find some enemies sleeping underground. Loud noises will wake them, so take a careful approach and try to sneak up on them.

GOAT SIMULATOR
TURTLE POWER
Find some famous turtles

1. FIND THE SEWER
On the "Goat City Bay" map, head towards the middle of the map and you'll see a small bridge. Just below the bridge is the sewer entrance.

2. FIND THE TURTLES
Head inside the sewer and turn left into a huge room. It's the Teenage Mutant Ninja Turtles! Well . . . almost, anyway.

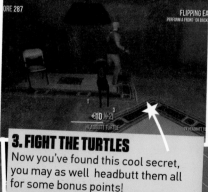

3. FIGHT THE TURTLES
Now you've found this cool secret, you may as well headbutt them all for some bonus points!

6 QUICK-FIRE ACHIEVEMENTS

SUPER TIME FORCE
THAT WAS QUICK

Die within three seconds of respawning

Given how manic the action is, you'll probably unlock this without even trying to.

DANGEROUS GOLF
DONE THIS BEFORE?

Trigger a Smashbreaker for the first time

You can do this with your very first shot in the game.

GRIM FANDANGO
"WHAT I DID BACK IN THE FAT DAYS IS NONE OF YOUR BUSINESS"

Talk to Eva about how she got stuck here

As soon as you start playing, ask Eva in the hall about her personal business.

BEYOND EYES
THOUGHTFUL

Feed the ducks

You'll get bread in Chapter 4. Cross the bridge and turn right to find and feed the ducks.

OLLIOLLI
DIZZY

Land a 540 Spin

You can do this on the very first jump of the very first stage.

STRIKE SUIT ZERO
SHOOT THE MOON

You can shoot the moon . . . we're just not telling you how

As soon as you can fire missiles in the opening mission, shoot the moon.

FEZ
A HIDDEN CUBE

Get an anti-cube with this code

Look in your Achievement or Trophy list and you'll find a code that will unlock one of the game's hidden anti-cubes. All you need to do is press the following buttons: R2, R2, L2, R2, R2, L2, L2, L2. Once you have entered the code, an anti-cube will appear above you and you simply need to jump to collect it.

FLOWER
MAKE IT BLOOM

How to make your flower reach its full potential

The game doesn't tell you this, but to make your flower bloom to its full potential, you need to find three secret flowers in each level (the small clumps of green flowers). Keep exploring until you find every one if you want to 100% complete the game.

NIDHOGG
EN GARDE!
Disarm your foe

To knock your opponent's sword out of their hand, you need to cross your swords when your sword is over half way past their sabre (this is easiest when they miss a lunge). For example, if your sword is in the high position and your opponent's is in the middle position, pressing down will disarm them.

DON'T STARVE: GIANT EDITION
WINTER IS COMING
Build a Thermal Stone

Making a Thermal Stone should be one of your key objectives as it will be a big help surviving the Winter season. Once you have an Alchemy Engine, collect ten stones, three flint, and one pickaxe to craft it. The stone can be heated and carried to keep you warm.

STARS OF THE FUTURE

PSYCHONAUTS 2
One of the indie titles we are most looking forward to playing is Double Fine's *Psychonauts 2*. If it's anything like the hilarious first game, it will be great.

CUPHEAD
This amazing game looks like a living cartoon from the Thirties. It has been delayed so the developer can add traditional levels to its boss battling core.

RIME
The beautiful puzzle platformer *Rime* looks to be influenced by games such as *Ico* and *The Legend of Zelda: Wind Waker*. That sounds like a recipe for success!

DIVEKICK ADDITION EDITION +
BECOME A CHAMPION

How to come out on top

This game is all about spacing, so it's very important that you practice with each character, as they all have different angles and ranges. Once you've got that down, patience is the most important skill to have. You are far better waiting for your opponent to make a mistake and then punishing them than playing very aggressively.

THE UNFINISHED SWAN
BALLOON COLLECTOR

Find every balloon in the game

Once you have collected three balloons, you are able to buy the Balloon Finder toy. This will let you know whenever you are near a balloon, making it far easier to find them all.

Press ⬤ to use telescope

EXTREME EXORCISM
LESS IS MORE

Shoot less, survive longer

When you defeat the main enemy of each round, a ghost appears in the next round that will copy every move you made in the previous round. Because of this, try to fire as few bullets as possible—otherwise there will be bullets flying all over the place in the next round, making it more difficult!

THE BANNER SAGA 2
OWN THE BATTLEFIELD

Become a tactical master of turn-based battles

1. Balance Is Key

It's important that you have a well-balanced party. Having a mix of roles, such as Varl, archers, and warriors is a good start. You should also pay attention to each character's unique abilities and how they can work together.

LOCOCYCLE
THE RIGHT CHOICES
The upgrades you need to succeed

The first ability you should upgrade is your ability to interrupt attacks when throwing Pablo. It becomes very useful late in the game. Regeneration is the next upgrade you should focus on—this will come in particularly handy during long boss fights where there are no health pickups. Stay still without boosting or firing to regenerate your health with this ability.

COUNTER

THE EXPERT SAYS . . .

Photo courtesy of Gareth Dutton

DAN PEARCE
GAME DIRECTOR, FOUR CIRCLE INT., DEVELOPERS OF 10 SECOND NINJA

Achievements allow the designer to address the player in a way that might seem strange in the game itself. For example, in *10 Second Ninja X*, the game's hub is a floating airship and it's possible for the player to jump off the front of it. We knew people were going to try and break the game by doing this, so we hid an Easter egg there. When the player jumps off, we trigger a secret Achievement called "AAAAAAAH!" and turn the notification into a kind of punch line. It acknowledges the player and says "we knew you were going to do that."

2. Collect Artifacts
Artifacts are items you can equip to give party members a boost. You can buy them in markets with Renown, but can often find them for free by stopping at Godstones.

4. Go Large
As a general rule, you should target the bigger and more powerful enemies first and leave weaker units. This will put you in a far stronger tactical position and should lead you on your way to victory.

3. Use Your Willpower
Don't be too cautious about using Willpower in battle to move further or hit harder. While you might be tempted to hold onto it, the longer a battle goes on, the more dangerous the fight can become.

MIGHTY NO. 9

This spiritual successor to the *Mega Man* series isn't just a homage to Capcom's classic games—it's actually created by the same person! Fans of the famously difficult *Mega Man* titles will feel right at home in this colorful new game.

TIPS & STRATEGY

BEGINNER ◄
GET IN, GET OUT

Weaken bosses with regular attacks, then dash into them to knock a chunk off their health. Just remember to dash back to safety afterwards!

BEAT BATTALION

Mighty No. 5, Battalion, should be your first target. The fight isn't that difficult and the weapon you get for winning is one of the best in the game.

INTERMEDIATE ◄◄
CROUCH DASH

By crouching before dashing, you make yourself a smaller target—perfect for when you're not entirely confident that you'll clear an attack.

EXPLOIT WEAKNESS

Each boss is particularly vulnerable to one of the unlockable weapons from another. Use this to your advantage for quick kills.

ADVANCED ◄◄◄
PICK YOUR BATTLES

When going for speed, don't stop to fight every enemy. You only need to attack those that halt progress, which should lead to speedier clears.

SOFT RESET

If a run isn't going to plan and it looks like you might run out of lives, simply quit out to the menu and start it again—this won't even add to your time for the speedrun Trophies!

CHEATS & SECRETS

UNLOCK CO-OP MODE

After beating all eight stages, you'll reach a prison level where you play as Call. Beat this stage to unlock co-op.

HARDER MODES

Clearing the game once opens up all the tougher difficulty levels, as well as New Game+ mode.

TOP 4
Achievements & Trophies

MIGHTY NO.

☺ WEIRDEST ACHIEVEMENT
WE CAN WORK IT OUT
Don't attack for the first 30 seconds of a boss battle
Learn the boss's attacks and practice dodging them if you want to unlock this challenging Achievement.

🏆 SECRET ACHIEVEMENT
MIGHTY ANNIVERSARY
Finish the game on the 9th
The only way you can unlock this Achievement or Trophy is by completing the game on the 9th of any month. Mark your diary and make sure you practice first.

💎 RAREST TROPHY
CLEARED STORY (SUPER FAST)
Complete the game within 60 minutes
Completing *Mighty No. 9* is tough. Completing *Mighty No. 9* within two hours is tougher. But completing *Mighty No. 9* within just one hour? That's a feat very few gamers have accomplished.

☻ COOLEST TROPHY
SELF-IMPOSED CHALLENGE
Defeat all bosses with normal attacks
Head into the menu and set the number of lives to nine to give you a better chance of pulling this one off.

TERRARIA

Fans of *Minecraft* will be right at home with this indie sensation, where you're free to create incredible structures, go on epic quests, and craft yourself some legendary gear. Do what you want, when you want, and have fun out there!

TIPS & STRATEGY

BEGINNER
IT GROWS ON TREES

Wood is the most basic and versatile resource in the early stages of a game, used to craft everything from shelter to equipment. Stock up early and don't run out.

BRING A FEW FRIENDS

The difficulty levels of enemies doesn't scale in line with the number of players, so recruiting friends can make even the trickiest bosses much more manageable.

INTERMEDIATE
STAR CATCHER

If you want to retrieve more fallen stars for additional mana, you can build bridges over large gaps or bodies of water. Watch out for roaming enemies when you're collecting them, though!

THE RESET STRATEGY

Random generation can be cruel! Once you have a decent grasp of the game, keep starting new games until you find a starting area you're happy with. A nearby meteorite or mineral reserve can be a great early boost.

ADVANCED
MOON MASTER

While difficult at first, Blood Moon events can be lucrative if you're prepared. Dig trenches on either side of your house to trap ground-based enemies and make the event easier.

CHEATS & SECRETS

SLIME ATTACK!
On the main page of terraria.org, input the Konami code to cause a wave of pesky slimes to invade your browser!

FLOATING ISLANDS
Rare items and materials spawn on the islands high above the world. Build a huge ladder to get to them.

TOP 4 Achievements & Trophies

⊙ EASIEST ACHIEVEMENT
TERRARIA STUDENT
You have begun the tutorial!
You get this just for booting up the tutorial at the start of the game—you don't even have to finish it! You might learn something, though . . .

☑ RAREST ACHIEVEMENT
EXTERMINATOR
You have defeated every boss
There are 13 bosses in the game, and six of those spawn only in Hard mode. This can be tricky because a lot of the bosses require a rare item to summon them, and *then* you have to defeat them.

⊙ COOLEST TROPHY
CROWD CONTROL
You have defeated the goblin army!
Once you've crafted the Goblin Battle Standard and have 200+ health, a massive horde of goblins will charge on your location. It's your job to take them out . . . all of them.

☗ SECRET TROPHY
APPEASE THE VOLCANO GODS
You sacrificed the Guide to boiling hot lava!
Dig down until you hit lava, fill a bucket with it, and make your way back to ground level. Find the Guide, dig a hole under him, block him in, and pour the lava on him.

HOW GOOD AT GAMES ARE YOU?

CAN YOU BEAT OUR FINAL CHALLENGE?

Playing your favorite games and unlocking all of their Achievements and Trophies is one thing. But do you have the skill to complete our list of challenges? Be warned—they might start off easy, but the final trials are mind-blowingly difficult. If you think of this book as a game, the next few pages are your final boss—the toughest gaming face-off you will ever experience. We've put together a collection of challenges so difficult that beating them will give you ultimate bragging rights among your friends. But don't worry, we haven't left you totally in the dark. Along with each test, we've added a few little tricks and cheats to help you . . .

FORZA MOTORSPORT 6

THRU THE PACK
Go from last place to first in a 24-player online race

If you're lucky, you'll land in a race where you easily outperform all your competitors' cars. In that case, just let yourself go into last place, then blast back up to first. Otherwise, you'll need some serious skills and patience.

MINECRAFT

SNIPER DUEL
Kill a skeleton with an arrow from more than 50 meters away

Being accurate enough to actually hit the skeleton is one thing. Stopping it from running at you, so it's closer than 50 meters, is another thing entirely. Do this one on the surface. Move slowly and sneak up on a skelly. Ideally, you need to have a bow powerful enough to take it down in one shot.

TRIALS FUSION

LEVEL UP
Reach "Floor 10" on The Tower

Floor 4
Be careful of the big concrete pillar. Make sure you hit it with the center of the bike, not the front or back wheel.

Floor 7
Keep accelerating and lean forward onto the bike, otherwise you'll flip over backwards.

Floor 10
Can you go that extra mile and make it to "Floor 11?" Anyone who can manage the back flip onto the pipe on this floor has our respect.

DON'T STARVE

THE SILENT
Unlock Wes "The Silent"

Once you reach the third stage of Adventure mode, look around until you find a statue of Maxwell. Destroy it, then defeat the enemies that spawn. Find another statue and repeat. Then search for the chamber where Wes is hiding. Defeat his guards and he's unlocked.

PLANTS VS. ZOMBIES GARDEN WARFARE 2

GOAT ANY LAST WORDS?
As a Goat, vanquish a Plant

This one is tough because you can't guarantee when you'll get turned into a goat. Even when you do get transformed, you won't do much damage. Try to time your attack so you strike the final blow . . .

LEGO STAR WARS: THE FORCE AWAKENS

THE NEW JEDI WILL RISE
Collect True Jedi on all the levels

Smash everything. Look in every crevice and corner. Each level requires that you find a different amount of studs, ranging from an easy 30,000 to an eye-watering 175,000. If you explore thoroughly, this one will be yours.

TEARAWAY UNFOLDED

TAXI!
Safely deliver the gopher back home

Collect the boulder at the start of "Chapter 6" and throw it at the screen. It'll bounce back and open the cracked cave wall. Inside is a gopher! If you pick him up and carry him through the whole level (you can put him down to fight) you'll unlock this cool secret Trophy.

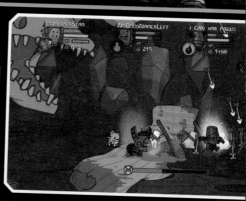

RATCHET & CLANK

GO SPEED RATCHET, GO!
Win the Gold Cup on both "Rilgar" and "Kalebo"

Don't hit your boost until it's all the way full, and remember that the hoverboard is pretty slippery—if you go into a corner too fast, you'll go screeching off, losing precious seconds. Hit every ramp you encounter and always stick close to the walls.

CASTLE CRASHERS REMASTERED

THE FINAL COUNTDOWN
Survive until 2:30 in a Back off Barbarian match

Let yourself fail at this twice (trust us) and you'll end up on a map with a forest area and a cliff at the top. There, you'll have a great bottleneck—enemies can still get to you, but only at a steady pace.

MEDIUM DIFFICULTY ★ MEDIUM D

1. MINE

You need to get digging. To build the rail itself you'll need 190 Iron Ingots. You'll also need 18 Gold Ingots and 22 Redstone Rust in order to make Powered Rails, which you'll place at various points on the track to push your cart along.

MINECRAFT

ON A RAIL
Travel by Minecart to a point at least 500 meters away from where you started

2. CLEAR

Back on the surface, you need to clear space for your track. Do it in a straight line (this is much quicker and simpler) and use the map to measure your track as you build it.

3. BUILD

Spread your Powered Rails thirty blocks apart, using the map to measure the distance, so you can stay at the same speed. If the cart stops and you have to push it, the Achievement won't count.

4. RIDE!

It's a good idea to start your rail at the top of a hill so you get a rolling start. Either give yourself a little push and then jump in, or get a friend to nudge you off the starting line.

SHOVEL KNIGHT

TRUE SHOVELRY
Complete the game without collecting any Relics

You better get some practice in, because this is tough. However, you can play on New Game, not New Game+, and the Trophy will still count. You can also still use Meal Tickets, Armor, and Shovel Skills. But you can't collect any Relics, which means no magic.

TERRARIA

TO HELL AND BACK
Travel to the Underworld and back without dying

Don't use a Magic Mirror—that won't count. Instead, dig a tunnel straight down to the Underworld and line it with wooden platforms so you can hop straight back up. You can die while building it, but as long as you go up and down in one life once it's finished, you're all good.

FIFA 16

PLAY BEAUTIFUL
Score a goal after making ten passes in a row in the opposing third of the field

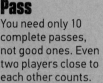

Position
Get in the enemy's eighteen-yard box. Try to have both wingers and your forward in space.

Pass
You need only 10 complete passes, not good ones. Even two players close to each other counts.

Finish
You don't want to nail all the passes, then mess up the goal. Play as a team with a great striker.

OVERWATCH

WHOA THERE!
Interrupt an enemy Ultimate ability with McCree's Flashbang

Timing is everything for this one. When you hear an Ultimate ability being used, quickly run in and throw it right at the opponent in question. The best characters to hit with this are Reaper, Symmetra, or a player using McCree on the other team.

HALO 5: GUARDIANS

FORGING A LEGEND
Complete every mission on Legendary difficulty

Co-op is a good idea for this one. Pick weapons that will complement each other. Having one person with an assault rifle and the other with a sniper is a strong combination. If you're feeling brave and want an extra 100G, you can go for the "Lone Wolf" Achievement at the same time: do every mission on Legendary alone.

HARD DIFFICULTY ★ HARD DIFFICULTY ★ HARD D

SPELUNKY

TO HELL AND BACK
Complete the game the hard way

1. The plan
You need to get into the secret "Hell" world and defeat its boss, King Yama. To do this, you'll have to complete several steps, all before fighting Olmec.

2. Udjat Eye
In the "Mines," find the golden key (it'll be obvious) and the golden treasure chest which it unlocks. Collect the Udjat Eye from the chest.

3. Black Market
In the "Jungle" levels, the Udjat Eye will flash and click when you are near the entrance to the "Black Market." Use bombs or a mattock to enter.

4. Ice Caves
In the "Black Market," buy or steal the Ankh. In the "Ice Caves," die near the big blue stone head and you'll respawn inside it to get the Hedjet helmet.

5. Temple
In the "Temple," find and kill Anubis (which takes two bombs), then collect his scepter. Use the sceptre on the golden locked door in the "City of Gold."

6. Olmec
Take the Book of the Dead to the "City of Gold." The book will writhe its face when you're above Hell. Get Olmec to jump onto this spot and you're in.

TIPS & TRICKS

PLAYSTATION TROPHIES
Playstationtrophies.org will not only help you figure out which Trophies you're missing, it will also tell you how to unlock them so you can complete your collection.

THE BIGGER THE GAME...
... the more Achievements. Huge games like *Minecraft* are full of Achievements, simply because there is so much to do.

STREET FIGHTER V

BACK FROM HELL
Win 100 fights in Survival Mode on Extreme difficulty

Make sure you pick the right supplements between battles and for the first ten fights at least. Save up all of your points, since things only get harder. Always try and land the first attack and finish with Critical or EX special moves.

DRIVECLUB

HOON-A-TIC

Rack up 1,000,000 Drift Points

Don't worry, you don't have to do this all in one race. But it's a long Achievement to unlock regardless. A recent patch means your Drift Points are now tracked in both online and offline modes, which is a bonus. You can also check how many you've racked up in the Progress menu.

ROCKET LEAGUE

SURVIVAL OF THE FITTEST

Equip the Shark Fin Topper and win an Unfair Bots match

You have to unlock the Shark Fin Topper, which is pretty easy through playing online. Then, enter Exhibition mode and change the Mutator settings so that Max Goal is at 1. This will put you in a 1 vs. 2 match. Stay tight on defense and only head toward the goal when your opponents are far from the ball.

PLANTS VS ZOMBIES: GARDEN WARFARE 2

INSANITY

Complete an ops game on Crazy Difficulty

Your best bet is to team up with three friends and to make sure one of you is playing as the Sunflower or Zombie Scientist, so you have a healer. Vampire Flower is a good perk as it replenishes your life for every kill.

HARD DIFFICULTY ★ HARD DIFFICU

FIFA 16

TAKE AIM
Achieve 100 percent shot accuracy in a match, with a minimum of ten shots

1. UP CLOSE AND PERSONAL

Take shots only from inside the eighteen-yard box. Don't use the volleys or headers, and play all of your corners and throw-ins short. You want to try and dribble right in front of goal, not take chances.

2. PLAY OFFENSIVE

Remember, you need to make ten shots, minimum, so don't hang back. Set the game timer to the longest possible to give you more time to set up attacks. Don't worry about winning as much as getting in those accurate shots.

OVERWATCH

SMOOTH AS SILK
Kill an enemy with a scoped headshot while airborne as Widowmaker

Wow. For a Bronze Trophy, this one really takes some skill. "King's Row" and "Watchpoint: Gibraltar" are the best maps for attempting this since they have the most ledges to jump from. Look for targets with low health and don't worry about fall damage.

STAR WARS BATTLEFRONT

MASTER
Complete all missions on Master difficulty

To unlock this Trophy, you need to complete four non-hero Battle missions, playing solo against the AI; four hero Battle missions solo against AI; and four Survival missions, which you can do solo, co-op, or online. Keep moving, in the non-hero Battle missions. For the hero missions, use Leia—she can heal herself!

DIFFICULTY ★ HARD DIFFICULTY ★ HA

3. SILKY SKILLS

If you can get around the goalkeeper, you're guaranteed a shot on target, if not an actual goal. Use the feint move (hold the right shoulder button, charge up a pass, and then at the last minute press shoot) to throw the keeper off balance and weave around him.

UNCHARTED: THE NATHAN DRAKE COLLECTION

UP A SHORT CREEK WITHOUT A PADDLE

In *Uncharted 1*, beat "Chapter 12" in less than five minutes

This is mainly a case of drilling the level into your head and resisting the urge to stop and shoot enemies. If you learn where the obstacles are and can hit them all in one or two tries, you'll be able to crack this one.

TITAN SOULS

ASCENSION

Collect all Trophies

Beat the game in "Iron Mode"? Beat the game without roll dodging? Beat the game in 20 MINUTES?! Think you can do this one? If so, you'd be one of the first. And you'll have truly earned your place as a video gaming legend. Good luck . . .

THE EXPERT SAYS . . .

RAY COX AKA STALLION83

First person to achieve a 1,000,000 Xbox Gamerscore

It was 2014 when Stallion83 did the unthinkable and finally achieved a Gamerscore of over 1,000,000, the big one million. As of right now, his GS is over 1,400,000. If you want to follow in his footsteps, Stallion's advice is trying and playing different games. Don't get too fixated on one single Achievement.

"I like keeping it fresh and going for the Achievements in a game when I'm ready, since going for some Achievements can be quite tedious. So playing another game, then coming back to an Achievement down the line is how I like to approach it. It keeps things fun and makes it less of a grind.

"I think the milestones of 10,000, 100,000, and so on are appealing. I like the idea of playing all the games and having those tied up and completed. I love it."

GLOSSARY

ESSENTIAL GAMING TERMS

ACHIEVEMENT

The name of the award you get for completing a specific task on Xbox platforms. Common examples of things that will reward you with an Achievement are finishing the game and finding a certain number of collectibles in the game levels.

ACHIEVEMENT HUNTER

A term that describes gamers who like to hunt down every Achievement that they can in games, in order to boost their overall Gamerscore.

BOOSTING

Getting friends to join you in an online match to let you win to boost your player stats or earn or unlock an Achievement or Trophy.

CAMPAIGN

Another word to describe the story of a game. For example, a single-player campaign is a series of pre-made maps and missions that you play on your own.

GLOSSARY

CAMPING

Sticking to one position in an online game, giving you a good view of the map or a key point without making you vulnerable. It can be frowned upon by other players.

CHEEVO

A shortened term for Achievement.

COMBO

A series of linked attacks that often requiring timing and skill. Most common in fighting games, but can apply to other genres, too.

CO-OP

A shorter term for cooperative play. This involves two or more players working together to achieve a common goal or objective.

CROWD CONTROL

A term used in online multiplayer games with lots of players, which refers to the ability to limit the number of enemies fighting during a specific encounter.

EASTER EGG

A joke, reference, or message deliberately hidden in a game. Sometimes, finding them can earn you an Achievement or Trophy.

EXPLOIT

Using a game system, bug, or glitch to your advantage in a way that isn't intended by the game's designers.

FARMING

The process of undertaking a repetitive task with a particular goal in mind, such as collecting a large number of a particular item.

GAME MECHANICS

The rules and systems that define how a game plays. This can include things such as hit points for characters. and movements.

GAMERSCORE

When you earn an Achievement in an Xbox game, you'll get points, or Gamerscore. These points are totalled to give you an overall Gamerscore, which will show on your profile. Also referred to as "G."

GRINDING

Refers to a tedious and repetitive action such as staying in one area and fighting monsters to level up your character. You might have to do this to get certain Achievements and Trophies!

HITBOX

An invisible area that defines when one thing hits another in a game. Characters can have a hitbox that roughly follows the character's design, but not exactly. You can appear to make contact with them without the game registering it.

INDIE GAMES

Games that are made by independent developers, usually with a small team, rather than large, established developers with hundreds of employees around the world.

INFLUENCER

An online gaming celebrity. Often used to refer to players who make videos or stream video games to their followers. They can "influence" fans by sharing their opinions on different games.

LEVEL CAP

The level cap is the highest level to which you can raise your character. Level caps are sometimes increased in later game updates.

MVP

Most valuable player. Usually used in online games.

GLITCHED ACHIEVEMENTS OR TROPHIES

A glitched Achievement or Trophy is one that isn't awarded to you when it should be, or that is rewarded to you even when you haven't completed the task you need to get it. These are usually fixed through game updates.

NEW GAME+

When you complete a game, a New Game+ mode can sometimes unlock. In most cases, you will keep all the abilities that you earned during your first play through, but the difficulty level in New Game+ is often higher.

NOOB

A new player. Also written as n00b. It is a shortened version of newbie.

NPC

Non-playable character.

PLAT

A shorter way to refer to a Platinum Trophy. Platinums can be unlocked only by getting every other Trophy in the game.

POACHING

The (generally frowned-upon) act of waiting until another player has completed a difficult task to then steal the benefits. For example, waiting for another player to do all the work defeating a boss and then jumping in to steal the item you get as a reward.

POPPED

When you say that an Achievement or Trophy has "popped," it means that the notification that tells you that you have unlocked it has appeared on the screen.

PROCEDURAL GENERATION

When a unique game world, or level, is made each time you play using a series of rules set by the developer. For example, every new Minecraft world is procedurally generated when you start a new game.

PVP

Player vs. player. This term is usually used in games that offer both a cooperative mode where you play together against computer controller characters, and competitive multiplayer where you play against other human players.

RAGEQUIT

When someone who is losing a multiplayer game quits before the match is over, usually out of frustration.

SHERPA

An experienced player who helps to guide new players through a game. You might need one to help you through a tough section of a game or to chase down the last few Achievement and Trophies you need!

SPEEDRUN

The practice of trying to complete a game as quickly as possible. Some speedruns make use of glitches and bugs to skip sections of the game, while others stick to playing the game as intended.

TROPHY

The name of the award you get for completing a specific task on PlayStation platforms. Trophies come in Bronze, Silver, Gold, and Platinum, depending on their difficulty.

TURTLING

Using a very defensive playstyle that can be easy to beat.

XP

Experience Points. Usually refers to in-game points that your character gains as you play. Earning a certain number will cause your character to level up and become more powerful. Reaching a certain level with your character can often be a criteria for unlocking Trophies and Achievements.